The UK Ninja Dual Zone Air Fryer Cookbook 2023

1500 Days Crispy and Energy-saving Recipes Elevate Your Cooking Game Will Love to Fry, Roast, Grill and Bake

Bess R. Harrison

Copyright © 2023 by Bess R. Harrison- All rights reserved.

The content contained within this book may not be reproduced, duplicated, or transmitted without direct written permission from the author or the publisher. Under no circumstances will any blame or legal responsibility be held against the publisher, or author, for any damages, reparation, or monetary loss due to the information contained within this book, either directly or indirectly.

Legal Notice: This book is copyright protected. It is only for personal use. You cannot amend, distribute, sell, use, quote or paraphrase any part, or the content within this book, without the consent of the author or publisher.

Disclaimer Notice: Please note the information contained within this document is for educational and entertainment purposes only. All effort has been executed to present accurate, up to date, reliable, complete information. No warranties of any kind are declared or implied. Readers acknowledge that the author is not engaged in the rendering of legal, financial, medical, or professional advice. The content within this book has been derived from various sources. Please consult a licensed professional before attempting any techniques outlined in this book. By reading this document, the reader agrees that under no circumstances is the author responsible for any losses, direct or indirect, that are incurred as a result of the use of the information contained within this document, including, but not limited to, errors, omissions, or inaccuracies

CONTENTS

INTRODUCTION I
What does this Air Fryer recipe book contain? I
What are the health benefits of the Air Fryer cookbook? II
How do Air Fryer recipes give convenience? III

Measurement Conversions IV

Breakfast Recipes 5
Cinnamon-raisin Bagels Everything Bagels 5
Banana And Raisins Muffins 6
Sweet Potato Hash 6
Baked Mushroom And Mozzarella Frittata With Breakfast Potatoes 7
Breakfast Potatoes 7
Sausage & Butternut Squash 8
Bacon And Eggs For Breakfast 8
Morning Egg Rolls 9
Air Fryer Sausage Patties 9
Yellow Potatoes With Eggs 10
Strawberry Baked Oats Chocolate Peanut Butter Baked Oats 10
Breakfast Sausage Omelet 11
Pumpkin French Toast Casserole With Sweet And Spicy Twisted Bacon 11
Perfect Cinnamon Toast 12
Breakfast Bacon 12
Cinnamon Toasts 13
Bagels 13
Bacon And Egg Omelet 14
Breakfast Casserole 14
Roasted Oranges 15
Blueberry Coffee Cake And Maple Sausage Patties 15
Egg With Baby Spinach 16
Spinach And Red Pepper Egg Cups With Coffee-glazed Canadian Bacon 17
Donuts 17

Snacks And Appetizers Recipes 18
Cauliflower Cheese Patties 18
Chicken Tenders 18
Parmesan French Fries 19
Kale Potato Nuggets 19
Crispy Plantain Chips 20
Mac And Cheese Balls 20
Onion Rings 21
Dried Apple Chips Dried Banana Chips 21
Cinnamon Sugar Chickpeas 22

Bacon Wrapped Tater Tots ... 22
Crispy Chickpeas ... 23
Grill Cheese Sandwich ... 23
Chili-lime Crispy Chickpeas Pizza-seasoned Crispy Chickpeas ... 24
Tater Tots ... 24
Crab Cakes ... 25
Parmesan Crush Chicken ... 25
Stuffed Bell Peppers ... 26
Tofu Veggie Meatballs ... 26
Jalapeño Popper Chicken ... 27
Crab Rangoon Dip With Crispy Wonton Strips ... 27
Avocado Fries With Sriracha Dip ... 28
Crab Cake Poppers ... 28
Jalapeño Popper Dip With Tortilla Chips ... 29
Mozzarella Balls ... 29

Beef, Pork, And Lamb Recipes ... 30

Lamb Shank With Mushroom Sauce ... 30
Pork Tenderloin With Brown Sugar–pecan Sweet Potatoes ... 30
Pork Chops And Potatoes ... 31
Pork Chops With Apples ... 31
Cilantro Lime Steak ... 32
Marinated Pork Chops ... 32
Strip Steaks With Hasselback Potatoes ... 33
Beef Ribs I ... 33
Curry-crusted Lamb Chops With Baked Brown Sugar Acorn Squash ... 34
Korean Bbq Beef ... 34
Ham Burger Patties ... 35
Yogurt Lamb Chops ... 35
Balsamic Steak Tips With Roasted Asparagus And Mushroom Medley ... 36
Sausage Meatballs ... 36
Pork Katsu With Seasoned Rice ... 37
Beef Ribs Ii ... 38
Lamb Chops With Dijon Garlic ... 38
Steak And Asparagus Bundles ... 39
Paprika Pork Chops ... 39
Pork With Green Beans And Potatoes ... 40
Bbq Pork Chops ... 40
Mongolian Beef With Sweet Chili Brussels Sprouts ... 41
Pork Chops With Brussels Sprouts ... 42
Tasty Pork Skewers ... 42

Poultry Recipes ... 43

Marinated Chicken Legs ... 43
Glazed Thighs With French Fries ... 43
Thai Chicken Meatballs ... 44
Italian Chicken & Potatoes ... 44
Bbq Cheddar-stuffed Chicken Breasts ... 45
Chicken And Potatoes ... 45
Cornish Hen ... 46

Ranch Turkey Tenders With Roasted Vegetable Salad 46
Balsamic Duck Breast 47
Chicken Parmesan 47
Veggie Stuffed Chicken Breasts 48
Wings With Corn On Cob 48
General Tso's Chicken 49
Juicy Duck Breast 49
Chicken Leg Piece 50
Yummy Chicken Breasts 50
Spicy Chicken Wings 51
Chicken & Veggies 51
Goat Cheese–stuffed Chicken Breast With Broiled Zucchini And Cherry Tomatoes 52
Honey-cajun Chicken Thighs 52
Roasted Garlic Chicken Pizza With Cauliflower "wings" 53
Bang-bang Chicken 53
Pickled Chicken Fillets 54
Spicy Chicken 54

Fish And Seafood Recipes 55

Buttered Mahi-mahi 55
Salmon With Green Beans 55
Parmesan-crusted Fish Sticks With Baked Macaroni And Cheese 56
Shrimp With Lemon And Pepper 56
Frozen Breaded Fish Fillet 57
Blackened Mahimahi With Honey-roasted Carrots 57
Flavorful Salmon With Green Beans 58
Spicy Salmon Fillets 58
Shrimp Skewers 58
Crispy Fish Nuggets 59
Broiled Teriyaki Salmon With Eggplant In Stir-fry Sauce 59
Crispy Parmesan Cod 60
Glazed Scallops 60
Savory Salmon Fillets 61
"fried" Fish With Seasoned Potato Wedges 61
Garlic Shrimp With Pasta Alfredo 62
Fried Tilapia 62
Southwestern Fish Fillets 63
Lemon Pepper Fish Fillets 63
Tuna Patties 64
Scallops 64
Fish Tacos 65
Tilapia With Mojo And Crispy Plantains 66
Shrimp Po'boys With Sweet Potato Fries 67

Vegetables And Sides Recipes 68

Garlic Potato Wedges In Air Fryer 68
Green Tomato Stacks 68
Veggie Burgers With "fried" Onion Rings 69
Fried Artichoke Hearts 70
Green Salad With Crispy Fried Goat Cheese And Baked Croutons 70

Buffalo Seitan With Crispy Zucchini Noodles ... 71
Acorn Squash Slices ... 71
Cheesy Potatoes With Asparagus ... 72
Lemon Herb Cauliflower ... 72
Falafel ... 73
Green Beans With Baked Potatoes ... 73
Lime Glazed Tofu ... 74
Chickpea Fritters ... 74
Bacon Wrapped Corn Cob ... 75
Air-fried Radishes ... 75
Potatoes & Beans ... 75
Hasselback Potatoes ... 76
Broccoli, Squash, & Pepper ... 76
Kale And Spinach Chips ... 77
Fried Olives ... 77
Delicious Potatoes & Carrots ... 78
Air Fried Okra ... 78
Sweet Potatoes & Brussels Sprouts ... 79
Fried Avocado Tacos ... 79

Desserts Recipes ... 80

Baked Apples ... 80
Monkey Bread ... 80
"air-fried" Oreos Apple Fries ... 81
Walnuts Fritters ... 82
Oreo Rolls ... 82
Grilled Peaches ... 83
Walnut Baklava Bites Pistachio Baklava Bites ... 83
Fudge Brownies ... 84
Chocolate Cookies ... 84
Jelly Donuts ... 85
Churros ... 85
Strawberry Nutella Hand Pies ... 86
Apple Nutmeg Flautas ... 86
Dehydrated Peaches ... 87
Air Fryer Sweet Twists ... 87
Brownie Muffins ... 87
Dessert Empanadas ... 88
Cake In The Air Fryer ... 88
Lemon Sugar Cookie Bars Monster Sugar Cookie Bars ... 89
Cinnamon Bread Twists ... 89
Lava Cake ... 90
Cinnamon-sugar "churros" With Caramel Sauce ... 90
Apple Fritters ... 91
Blueberry Pie Egg Rolls ... 91

Appendix : Recipes Index ... 92

INTRODUCTION

Welcome to Bess R. Harrison's Ninja Dual Zone Air Fryer Cookbook! Bess is a passionate home cook and a firm believer in the idea that nutritious meals should not come at the expense of taste or enjoyment.

If you're holding this book, it's likely you have a Air Fryer sitting in your kitchen, or perhaps you're contemplating getting one. Either way, this cookbook is your golden ticket to a world of gastronomic delights, all made simpler, healthier, and more accessible with this phenomenal appliance.

Inside, you'll discover a wide array of sumptuous recipes that are as nutritious as they are mouthwatering. From hearty breakfasts that'll kick-start your day, to succulent dinners that you'll be excited to share with family and friends, we've got you covered. And let's not forget about the scrumptious desserts and finger-licking good snacks!

But this cookbook is more than just a collection of recipes. It's about embracing a new way of cooking and eating. It's about experiencing the joy of creating meals that not only satisfy your palate but also contribute positively to your health. By utilizing Air Fryer, you're choosing a method of cooking that significantly reduces unhealthy fats without compromising on the flavor or the cherished crispy finish.

So, whether you're a seasoned cook or a novice in the kitchen, this cookbook is designed to inspire, guide, and transform your culinary adventures. Ready to tie on that apron and unleash the full potential of your Air Fryer? Let's dive in!"

What does this Air Fryer recipe book contain?

Breakfast Food Recipes

Bacon, Toasted bread, Omelettes or frittatas, Air-fried hash browns, French toast sticks

Lunch and Dinner Recipes

Grilled chicken, pork, or steak, Salmon or other types of fish, Crispy tofu, Stuffed bell peppers, Pizza, Air-fried meatballs, Veggie burgers, Shrimp skewers

Side Dishes and Snacks Recipes

French fries, Sweet potato fries, Zucchini or carrot chips, Crispy Brussels sprouts or cauliflower, Roasted asparagus, Mozzarella sticks, Jalapeno poppers

Baked Goods Recipes

Muffins, Cupcakes, Brownies, Cookies, Donuts

Desserts Recipes

Apple or other fruit fritters, Churros, Air-fried banana slices (great on top of ice cream!), Mini pies or tarts

In addition to this, the cookbook contains many delicious food recipes, all waiting for you to explore!

What are the health benefits of the Air Fryer cookbook?

Lower Fat Content

One of the primary benefits of Air Fryer is that it requires significantly less oil than traditional frying methods. This can lead to a significant reduction in the fat content of your meals, helping to lower your intake of unhealthy fats and calories.

Promotion of Healthy Eating

Many air fryer cookbooks include a range of recipes that utilize whole, nutrient-dense foods. This can encourage a more balanced diet, which is essential for overall health.

Reduced Acrylamide Intake

Acrylamide is a potentially harmful compound that can form in certain foods during high-temperature cooking, such as frying. Air Fryer has been shown to produce less acrylamide than traditional frying, which can potentially reduce your exposure to this compound.

Weight Management

By providing a lower-fat method of cooking, an Air Fryer cookbook can aid in weight management. Combined with portion control and regular exercise, it can be a helpful tool for those trying to lose or maintain their weight.

Improved Digestion

Many Air Fryer cookbooks include recipes for fiber-rich vegetables and whole grains. These foods can help improve your digestive health.

Reduced Sodium

You have the control over the amount of salt added to your food. With home-cooked Air Fryer meals, you can regulate and lower your sodium intake, which is beneficial for heart health.

How do Air Fryer recipes give convenience?

Air Fryers have become a popular appliance in many kitchens due to the numerous benefits they offer, including:

- **Healthier Meals**

Air Fryers use the circulation of hot air to cook food, which requires significantly less oil than traditional deep frying. This can result in meals with lower fat and calorie content, contributing to a healthier diet.

- **Fast and Efficient**

Because Air Fryers heat up very quickly, food can be cooked faster than in a traditional oven. This can save you time, particularly if you're cooking in large quantities.

- **Versatile Cooking Options**

Air Fryers can be used to fry, grill, bake, and roast, making them incredibly versatile. You can make a wide variety of foods, from chicken and fries to vegetables, seafood, and even baked goods.

- **Easy Clean-Up**

Most Air Fryers have removable, dishwasher-safe parts, making clean-up quick and easy. Additionally, because they use less oil, you won't have to deal with the greasy mess often associated with traditional frying.

- **Safer Than Deep Frying**

Deep frying at home can be risky due to the potential for oil splatter. Air Fryers eliminate this risk, as they cook food without the need for large amounts of hot, splattering oil.

- **Taste**

While they might not offer the exact taste and texture of deep-fried foods, Air Fryers do an excellent job of creating a crispy exterior and juicy interior, delivering a similar experience with less oil.

- **Space-Saving**

Air Fryers are compact appliances that can easily fit on your kitchen counter, saving space compared to larger appliances like ovens.

Measurement Conversions

BASIC KITCHEN CONVERSIONS & EQUIVALENTS

DRY MEASUREMENTS CONVERSION CHART

3 TEASPOONS = 1 TABLESPOON = 1/16 CUP

6 TEASPOONS = 2 TABLESPOONS = 1/8 CUP

12 TEASPOONS = 4 TABLESPOONS = 1/4 CUP

24 TEASPOONS = 8 TABLESPOONS = 1/2 CUP

36 TEASPOONS = 12 TABLESPOONS = 3/4 CUP

48 TEASPOONS = 16 TABLESPOONS = 1 CUP

METRIC TO US COOKING CONVERSIONS

OVEN TEMPERATURES

120 °C = 250 °F

160 °C = 320 °F

180° C = 350 °F

205 °C = 400 °F

220 °C = 425 °F

LIQUID MEASUREMENTS CONVERSION CHART

8 FLUID OUNCES = 1 CUP = 1/2 PINT = 1/4 QUART

16 FLUID OUNCES = 2 CUPS = 1 PINT = 1/2 QUART

32 FLUID OUNCES = 4 CUPS = 2 PINTS = 1 QUART

 = 1/4 GALLON

128 FLUID OUNCES = 16 CUPS = 8 PINTS = 4 QUARTS = 1 GALLON

BAKING IN GRAMS

1 CUP FLOUR = 140 GRAMS

1 CUP SUGAR = 150 GRAMS

1 CUP POWDERED SUGAR = 160 GRAMS

1 CUP HEAVY CREAM = 235 GRAMS

VOLUME

1 MILLILITER = 1/5 TEASPOON

5 ML = 1 TEASPOON

15 ML = 1 TABLESPOON

240 ML = 1 CUP OR 8 FLUID OUNCES

1 LITER = 34 FL. OUNCES

WEIGHT

1 GRAM = .035 OUNCES

100 GRAMS = 3.5 OUNCES

500 GRAMS = 1.1 POUNDS

1 KILOGRAM = 35 OUNCES

US TO METRIC COOKING CONVERSIONS

1/5 TSP = 1 ML

1 TSP = 5 ML

1 TBSP = 15 ML

1 FL OUNCE = 30 ML

1 CUP = 237 ML

1 PINT (2 CUPS) = 473 ML

1 QUART (4 CUPS) = .95 LITER

1 GALLON (16 CUPS) = 3.8 LITERS

1 OZ = 28 GRAMS

1 POUND = 454 GRAMS

BUTTER

1 CUP BUTTER = 2 STICKS = 8 OUNCES = 230 GRAMS = 8 TABLESPOONS

WHAT DOES 1 CUP EQUAL

1 CUP = 8 FLUID OUNCES

1 CUP = 16 TABLESPOONS

1 CUP = 48 TEASPOONS

1 CUP = 1/2 PINT

1 CUP = 1/4 QUART

1 CUP = 1/16 GALLON

1 CUP = 240 ML

BAKING PAN CONVERSIONS

1 CUP ALL-PURPOSE FLOUR = 4.5 OZ

1 CUP ROLLED OATS = 3 OZ 1 LARGE EGG = 1.7 OZ

1 CUP BUTTER = 8 OZ 1 CUP MILK = 8 OZ

1 CUP HEAVY CREAM = 8.4 OZ

1 CUP GRANULATED SUGAR = 7.1 OZ

1 CUP PACKED BROWN SUGAR = 7.75 OZ

1 CUP VEGETABLE OIL = 7.7 OZ

1 CUP UNSIFTED POWDERED SUGAR = 4.4 OZ

BAKING PAN CONVERSIONS

9-INCH ROUND CAKE PAN = 12 CUPS

10-INCH TUBE PAN = 16 CUPS

11-INCH BUNDT PAN = 12 CUPS

9-INCH SPRINGFORM PAN = 10 CUPS

9 X 5 INCH LOAF PAN = 8 CUPS

9-INCH SQUARE PAN = 8 CUPS

Breakfast Recipes

Cinnamon-raisin Bagels Everything Bagels

Servings:4
Cooking Time: 14 Minutes

Ingredients:
- FOR THE BAGEL DOUGH
- 1 cup all-purpose flour, plus more for dusting
- 2 teaspoons baking powder
- 1 teaspoon kosher salt
- 1 cup reduced-fat plain Greek yogurt
- FOR THE CINNAMON-RAISIN BAGELS
- ¼ cup raisins
- ½ teaspoon ground cinnamon
- FOR THE EVERYTHING BAGELS
- ¼ teaspoon poppy seeds
- ¼ teaspoon sesame seeds
- ¼ teaspoon dried minced garlic
- ¼ teaspoon dried minced onion
- FOR THE EGG WASH
- 1 large egg
- 1 tablespoon water

Directions:
1. To prep the bagels: In a large bowl, combine the flour, baking powder, and salt. Stir in the yogurt to form a soft dough. Turn the dough out onto a lightly floured surface and knead five to six times, until it is smooth and elastic. Divide the dough in half.
2. Knead the raisins and cinnamon into one dough half. Leave the other dough half plain.
3. Divide both portions of dough in half to form a total of 4 balls of dough (2 cinnamon-raisin and 2 plain). Roll each ball of dough into a rope about 8 inches long. Shape each rope into a ring and pinch the ends to seal.
4. To prep the everything bagels: In a small bowl, mix together the poppy seeds, sesame seeds, garlic, and onion.
5. To prep the egg wash: In a second small bowl, beat together the egg and water. Brush the egg wash on top of each bagel.
6. Generously sprinkle the everything seasoning over the top of the 2 plain bagels.
7. To cook the bagels: Install a crisper plate in each of the two baskets. Place the cinnamon-raisin bagels in the Zone 1 basket and insert the basket in the unit. For best results, the bagels should not overlap in the basket. Place the everything bagels in the Zone 2 basket and insert the basket in the unit.
8. Select Zone 1, select AIR FRY, set the temperature to 325°F, and set the time to 14 minutes. Select MATCH COOK to match Zone 2 settings to Zone 1.
9. Press START/PAUSE to begin cooking.
10. When cooking is complete, use silicone-tipped tongs to transfer the bagels to a cutting board. Let cool for 2 to 3 minutes before cutting and serving.

Nutrition Info:
- (Per serving) Calories: 238; Total fat: 3g; Saturated fat: 1g; Carbohydrates: 43g; Fiber: 1.5g; Protein: 11g; Sodium: 321mg

Banana And Raisins Muffins

Servings: 2
Cooking Time: 16

Ingredients:
- Salt, pinch
- 2 eggs, whisked
- 1/3 cup butter, melted
- 4 tablespoons of almond milk
- ¼ teaspoon of vanilla extract
- ½ teaspoon of baking powder
- 1-1/2 cup all-purpose flour
- 1 cup mashed bananas
- 2 tablespoons of raisins

Directions:
1. Take about 4 large (one-cup sized) ramekins and layer them with muffin papers.
2. Crack eggs in a large bowl, and whisk it all well and start adding vanilla extract, almond milk, baking powder, and melted butter
3. Whisk the ingredients very well.
4. Take a separate bowl and add the all-purpose flour, and salt.
5. Now, combine the add dry ingredients with the wet ingredients.
6. Now, pour mashed bananas and raisins into this batter
7. Mix it well to make a batter for the muffins.
8. Now pour the batter into four ramekins and divided the ramekins in the air fryer zones.
9. Set the timer for zone 1 to 16 minutes at 350 degrees F.
10. Select the MATCH button for the zone 2 basket.
11. Check if not done, and let it AIR FRY for one more minute.
12. Once it is done, serve.

Nutrition Info:
- (Per serving) Calories 727| Fat 43.1g| Sodium366 mg | Carbs 74.4g | Fiber 4.7g | Sugar 16.1g | Protein 14.1g

Sweet Potato Hash

Servings: 4
Cooking Time: 15 Minutes

Ingredients:
- 3 sweet potatoes, peel & cut into ½-inch pieces
- ½ tsp cinnamon
- 2 tbsp olive oil
- 1 bell pepper, cut into ½-inch pieces
- ½ tsp dried thyme
- ½ tsp nutmeg
- 1 medium onion, cut into ½-inch pieces
- Pepper
- Salt

Directions:
1. In a bowl, toss sweet potatoes with the remaining ingredients.
2. Insert a crisper plate in Ninja Foodi air fryer baskets.
3. Add potato mixture in both baskets.
4. Select zone 1 then select "air fry" mode and set the temperature to 355 degrees F for 15 minutes. Press "match" to match zone 2 settings to zone 1. Press "start/stop" to begin.

Nutrition Info:
- (Per serving) Calories 167 | Fat 7.3g |Sodium 94mg | Carbs 24.9g | Fiber 4.2g | Sugar 6.8g | Protein 2.2g

Baked Mushroom And Mozzarella Frittata With Breakfast Potatoes

Servings: 4
Cooking Time: 35 Minutes
Ingredients:
- FOR THE FRITTATA
- 8 large eggs
- ⅓ cup whole milk
- 1 teaspoon kosher salt
- ½ teaspoon freshly ground black pepper
- 1 cup sliced cremini mushrooms (about 2 ounces)
- 1 teaspoon olive oil
- 2 ounces part-skim mozzarella cheese, cut into ½-inch cubes
- FOR THE POTATOES
- 2 russet potatoes, cut into ½-inch cubes
- 1 tablespoon olive oil
- ½ teaspoon garlic powder
- ¼ teaspoon kosher salt
- ¼ teaspoon freshly ground black pepper

Directions:
1. To prep the frittata: In a large bowl, whisk together the eggs, milk, salt, and pepper. Stir in the mushrooms.
2. To prep the potatoes: In a large bowl, combine the potatoes, olive oil, garlic powder, salt, and black pepper.
3. To cook the frittata and potatoes: Brush the bottom of the Zone 1 basket with 1 teaspoon of olive oil. Add the egg mixture to the basket, top with the mozzarella cubes, and insert the basket in the unit. Install a crisper plate in the Zone 2 basket. Place the potatoes in the basket and insert the basket in the unit.
4. Select Zone 1, select BAKE, set the temperature to 350°F, and set the time to 30 minutes.
5. Select Zone 2, select AIR FRY, set the temperature to 400°F, and set the time to 35 minutes. Select SMART FINISH.
6. Press START/PAUSE to begin cooking.
7. When the Zone 2 timer reads 15 minutes, press START/PAUSE. Remove the basket and shake the potatoes for 10 seconds. Reinsert the basket and press START/PAUSE to resume cooking.
8. When cooking is complete, the frittata will pull away from the edges of the basket and the potatoes will be golden brown. Transfer the frittata to a cutting board and cut into 4 portions. Serve with the potatoes.

Nutrition Info:
- (Per serving) Calories: 307; Total fat: 17g; Saturated fat: 5.5g; Carbohydrates: 18g; Fiber: 1g; Protein: 19g; Sodium: 600mg

Breakfast Potatoes

Servings: 6
Cooking Time: 20 Minutes
Ingredients:
- 3 potatoes, peeled and diced
- 1 onion yellow, diced
- 1 green pepper diced
- 2 teaspoons salt
- ½ teaspoon pepper
- 2 tablespoons olive oil
- 1 cup cheese shredded

Directions:
1. Toss potatoes with onion, green peppers, black pepper, salt and cheese in a bowl.
2. Divide the potato mixture into the Ninja Foodi 2 Baskets Air Fryer baskets.
3. Return the air fryer basket 1 to Zone 1, and basket 2 to Zone 2 of the Ninja Foodi 2-Basket Air Fryer.
4. Choose the "Air Fry" mode for Zone 1 at 400 degrees F temperature and 20 minutes of cooking time.
5. Select the "MATCH COOK" option to copy the settings for Zone 2.
6. Initiate cooking by pressing the START/PAUSE BUTTON.
7. Toss the veggies once cooked halfway through.
8. Serve warm.

Nutrition Info:
- (Per serving) Calories 209 | Fat 7.5g | Sodium 321mg | Carbs 34.1g | Fiber 4g | Sugar 3.8g | Protein 4.3g

Sausage & Butternut Squash

Servings: 2
Cooking Time: 20 Minutes

Ingredients:
- 450g butternut squash, diced
- 70g kielbasa, diced
- ¼ onion, diced
- ¼ tsp garlic powder
- ½ tbsp olive oil
- Pepper
- Salt

Directions:
1. In a bowl, toss butternut squash with garlic powder, oil, onion, kielbasa, pepper, and salt.
2. Insert a crisper plate in the Ninja Foodi air fryer baskets.
3. Add sausage and butternut squash mixture in both baskets.
4. Select zone 1, then select "air fry" mode and set the temperature to 375 degrees F for 20 minutes. Press "match" to match zone 2 settings to zone 1. Press "start/stop" to begin. Stir halfway through.

Nutrition Info:
- (Per serving) Calories 68 | Fat 3.6g | Sodium 81mg | Carbs 9.7g | Fiber 1.7g | Sugar 2.2g | Protein 0.9g

Bacon And Eggs For Breakfast

Servings: 1
Cooking Time: 12

Ingredients:
- 4 strips of thick-sliced bacon
- 2 small eggs
- Salt and black pepper, to taste
- Oil spray for greasing ramekins

Directions:
1. Take 2 ramekins and grease them with oil spray.
2. Crack eggs in a bowl and season it salt and black pepper.
3. Divide the egg mixture between two ramekins.
4. Put the bacon slices into Ninja Foodie 2-Basket Air Fryer zone 1 basket, and ramekins in zone 2 baskets.
5. Now for zone 1 set it to AIR FRY mode at 400 degrees F for 12 minutes.
6. And for zone 2 set it 350 degrees for 8 minutes using AIR FRY mode.
7. Press the Smart finish button and press start, it will finish both at the same time.
8. Once done, serve and enjoy.

Nutrition Info:
- (Per serving) Calories 131 | Fat 10g | Sodium 187mg | Carbs 0.6 g | Fiber 0g | Sugar 0.6g | Protein 10.7

Morning Egg Rolls

Servings: 6
Cooking Time: 13 Minutes.

Ingredients:
- 2 eggs
- 2 tablespoons milk
- Salt, to taste
- Black pepper, to taste
- ½ cup shredded cheddar cheese
- 2 sausage patties
- 6 egg roll wrappers
- 1 tablespoon olive oil
- 1 cup water

Directions:
1. Grease a small skillet with some olive oil and place it over medium heat.
2. Add sausage patties and cook them until brown.
3. Chop the cooked patties into small pieces. Beat eggs with salt, black pepper, and milk in a mixing bowl.
4. Grease the same skillet with 1 teaspoon of olive oil and pour the egg mixture into it.
5. Stir cook to make scrambled eggs.
6. Add sausage, mix well and remove the skillet from the heat.
7. Spread an egg roll wrapper on the working surface in a diamond shape position.
8. Add a tablespoon of cheese at the bottom third of the roll wrapper.
9. Top the cheese with egg mixture and wet the edges of the wrapper with water.
10. Fold the two corners of the wrapper and roll it, then seal the edges.
11. Repeat the same steps and divide the rolls in the two crisper plates.
12. Return the crisper plates to the Ninja Foodi Dual Zone Air Fryer.
13. Choose the Air Fry mode for Zone 1 and set the temperature to 375 degrees F and the time to 13 minutes.
14. Select the "MATCH" button to copy the settings for Zone 2.
15. Initiate cooking by pressing the START/STOP button.
16. Flip the rolls after 8 minutes and continue cooking for another 5 minutes.
17. Serve warm and fresh.

Nutrition Info:
- (Per serving) Calories 282 | Fat 15g | Sodium 526mg | Carbs 20g | Fiber 0.6g | Sugar 3.3g | Protein 16g

Air Fryer Sausage Patties

Servings: 12
Cooking Time: 10 Minutes

Ingredients:
- 1-pound pork sausage or ready-made patties
- Fennel seeds or preferred seasonings

Directions:
1. Prepare the sausage by slicing it into patties, then flavor it with fennel seed or your favorite seasonings.
2. Install a crisper plate in both drawers. Place half the patties in zone 1 and half in zone 2, then insert the drawers into the unit.
3. Select zone 1, select AIR FRY, set temperature to 390 degrees F/ 200 degrees C, and set time to 10 minutes.
4. Select MATCH to match zone 2 settings to zone 1.
5. Press the START/STOP button to begin cooking.
6. When cooking is complete, remove the patties from the unit and serve with sauce or make a burger.

Nutrition Info:
- (Per serving) Calories 130 | Fat 10.5g | Sodium 284mg | Carbs 0.3g | Fiber 0.2g | Sugar 0g | Protein 7.4g

Yellow Potatoes With Eggs

Servings: 2
Cooking Time: 35

Ingredients:

- 1 pound of Dutch yellow potatoes, quartered
- 1 red bell pepper, chopped
- Salt and black pepper, to taste
- 1 green bell pepper, chopped
- 2 teaspoons of olive oil
- 2 teaspoons of garlic powder
- 1 teaspoon of onion powder
- 1 egg
- ¼ teaspoon of butter

Directions:

1. Toss together diced potatoes, green pepper, red pepper, salt, black pepper, and olive oil along with garlic powder and onion powder.
2. Put in the zone 1 basket of the air fryer.
3. Take ramekin and grease it with oil spray.
4. Whisk egg in a bowl and add salt and pepper along with ½ teaspoon of butter.
5. Pour egg into a ramekin and place it in a zone 2 basket.
6. Now start cooking and set a timer for zone 1 basket to 30-35 minutes at 400 degrees at AIR FRY mode.
7. Now for zone 2, set it on AIR FRY mode at 350 degrees F for 8-10 minutes.
8. Press the Smart finish button and press start, it will finish both at the same time.
9. Once done, serve and enjoy.

Nutrition Info:

- (Per serving) Calories252 | Fat7.5g | Sodium 37mg | Carbs 40g | Fiber3.9g | Sugar 7g | Protein 6.7g

Strawberry Baked Oats Chocolate Peanut Butter Baked Oats

Servings: 12
Cooking Time: 15 Minutes

Ingredients:

- FOR THE STRAWBERRY OATS
- 1 cup whole milk
- 1 cup heavy (whipping) cream
- ½ cup maple syrup
- 2 teaspoons vanilla extract
- 2 large eggs
- 2 cups old-fashioned oats
- 2 teaspoons baking powder
- ½ teaspoon ground cinnamon
- ¼ teaspoon kosher salt
- 1½ cups diced strawberries
- FOR THE CHOCOLATE PEANUT BUTTER OATS
- 2 very ripe bananas
- ½ cup maple syrup
- ¼ cup unsweetened cocoa powder
- 2 teaspoons vanilla extract
- 2 teaspoons baking powder
- 2 large eggs
- ½ teaspoon kosher salt
- 2 cups old-fashioned oats
- 2 tablespoons peanut butter

Directions:

1. To prep the strawberry oats: In a large bowl, combine the milk, cream, maple syrup, vanilla, and eggs. Stir in the oats, baking powder, cinnamon, and salt until fully combined. Fold in the strawberries.
2. To prep the chocolate peanut butter oats: In a large bowl, mash the banana with a fork. Stir in the maple syrup, cocoa powder, vanilla, baking powder, and salt until smooth. Beat in the eggs. Stir in the oats until everything is combined.
3. To bake the oats: Place the strawberry oatmeal in the Zone 1 basket and insert the basket in the unit. Place the chocolate peanut butter oatmeal in the Zone 2 basket. Add ½ teaspoon dollops of peanut butter on top and insert the basket in the unit.
4. Select Zone 1, select BAKE, set the temperature to 320°F, and set the time to 15 minutes. Select MATCH COOK to match Zone 2 settings to Zone 1.
5. Press START/PAUSE to begin cooking.
6. When cooking is complete, serve each oatmeal in a shallow bowl.

Nutrition Info:

- (Per serving) Calories: 367; Total fat: 19g; Saturated fat: 11g; Carbohydrates: 42g; Fiber: 3.5g; Protein: 8g; Sodium: 102mg

Breakfast Sausage Omelet

Servings: 2
Cooking Time: 8

Ingredients:

- ¼ pound breakfast sausage, cooked and crumbled
- 4 eggs, beaten
- ½ cup pepper Jack cheese blend
- 2 tablespoons green bell pepper, sliced
- 1 green onion, chopped
- 1 pinch cayenne pepper
- Cooking spray

Directions:

1. Take a bowl and whisk eggs in it along with crumbled sausage, pepper Jack cheese, green onions, red bell pepper, and cayenne pepper.
2. Mix it all well.
3. Take two cake pans that fit inside the air fryer and grease it with oil spray.
4. Divide the omelet mixture between cake pans.
5. Put the cake pans inside both of the Ninja Foodie 2-Basket Air Fryer baskets.
6. Turn on the BAKE function of the zone 1 basket and let it cook for 15-20 minutes at 310 degrees F.
7. Select MATCH button for zone 2 basket.
8. Once the cooking cycle completes, take out, and serve hot, as a delicious breakfast.

Nutrition Info:

- (Per serving) Calories 691| Fat52.4g | Sodium1122 mg | Carbs 13.3g | Fiber 1.8g| Sugar 7g | Protein 42g

Pumpkin French Toast Casserole With Sweet And Spicy Twisted Bacon

Servings: 4
Cooking Time: 35 Minutes

Ingredients:

- FOR THE FRENCH TOAST CASSEROLE
- 3 large eggs
- 1 cup unsweetened almond milk
- 1 cup canned unsweetened pumpkin puree
- 2 teaspoons pumpkin pie spice
- ¼ cup packed light brown sugar
- 1 teaspoon vanilla extract
- 6 cups French bread cubes
- 1 teaspoon vegetable oil
- ¼ cup maple syrup
- FOR THE BACON
- 2 tablespoons light brown sugar
- ⅛ teaspoon cayenne pepper
- 8 slices bacon

Directions:

1. To prep the French toast casserole: In a shallow bowl, whisk together the eggs, almond milk, pumpkin puree, pumpkin pie spice, brown sugar, and vanilla.
2. Add the bread cubes to the egg mixture, making sure the bread is fully coated in the custard. Let sit for at least 10 minutes to allow the bread to soak up the custard.
3. To prep the bacon: In a small bowl, combine the brown sugar and cayenne.
4. Arrange the bacon on a cutting board in a single layer. Evenly sprinkle the strips with the brown sugar mixture. Fold the bacon strip in half lengthwise. Hold one end of the bacon steady and twist the other end so the bacon resembles a straw.
5. To cook the casserole and bacon: Brush the Zone 1 basket with the oil. Pour the French toast casserole into the Zone 1 basket, drizzle with maple syrup, and insert the basket in the unit. Install a crisper plate in the Zone 2 basket, add the bacon twists in a single layer, and insert the basket in the unit. For the best fit, arrange the bacon twists across the unit, front to back.
6. Select Zone 1, select BAKE, set the temperature to 330°F, and set the time to 35 minutes.
7. Select Zone 2, select AIR FRY, set the temperature to 400°F, and set the time to 12 minutes. Select SMART FINISH.
8. Press START/PAUSE to begin cooking.
9. When cooking is complete, transfer the bacon to a plate lined with paper towels. Let cool for 2 to 3 minutes before serving with the French toast casserole.

Nutrition Info:

- (Per serving) Calories: 601; Total fat: 28g; Saturated fat: 9g; Carbohydrates: 67g; Fiber: 2.5g; Protein: 17g; Sodium: 814mg

Perfect Cinnamon Toast

Servings: 6
Cooking Time: 10 Minutes
Ingredients:

- 12 slices whole-wheat bread
- 1 stick butter, room temperature
- ½ cup white sugar
- 1½ teaspoons ground cinnamon
- 1½ teaspoons pure vanilla extract
- 1 pinch kosher salt
- 2 pinches freshly ground black pepper (optional)

Directions:
1. Mash the softened butter with a fork or the back of a spoon in a bowl. Add the sugar, cinnamon, vanilla, and salt. Stir until everything is well combined.
2. Spread one-sixth of the mixture onto each slice of bread, making sure to cover the entire surface.
3. Install a crisper plate in both drawers. Place half the bread sliced in the zone 1 drawer and half in the zone 2 drawer, then insert the drawers into the unit.
4. Select zone 1, select AIR FRY, set temperature to 400 degrees F/ 200 degrees C, and set time to 5 minutes. Select MATCH to match zone 2 settings to zone 1. Press theSTART/STOP button to begin cooking
5. When cooking is complete, remove the slices and cut them diagonally.
6. Serve immediately.

Nutrition Info:
- (Per serving) Calories 322 | Fat 16.5g | Sodium 249mg | Carbs 39.3g | Fiber 4.2g | Sugar 18.2g | Protein 8.2g

Breakfast Bacon

Servings: 4
Cooking Time: 14 Minutes.
Ingredients:

- ½ lb. bacon slices

Directions:
1. Spread half of the bacon slices in each of the crisper plate evenly in a single layer.
2. Return the crisper plate to the Ninja Foodi Dual Zone Air Fryer.
3. Choose the Air Fry mode for Zone 1 and set the temperature to 390 degrees F and the time to 14 minutes.
4. Select the "MATCH" button to copy the settings for Zone 2.
5. Initiate cooking by pressing the START/STOP button.
6. Flip the crispy bacon once cooked halfway through, then resume cooking.
7. Serve.

Nutrition Info:
- (Per serving) Calories 273 | Fat 22g |Sodium 517mg | Carbs 3.3g | Fiber 0.2g | Sugar 1.4g | Protein 16.1g

Cinnamon Toasts

Servings: 4
Cooking Time: 8 Minutes.

Ingredients:
- 4 pieces of bread
- 2 tablespoons butter
- 2 eggs, beaten
- 1 pinch salt
- 1 pinch cinnamon ground
- 1 pinch nutmeg ground
- 1 pinch ground clove
- 1 teaspoon icing sugar

Directions:
1. Add two eggs to a mixing bowl and stir cinnamon, nutmeg, ground cloves, and salt, then whisk well.
2. Spread butter on both sides of the bread slices and cut them into thick strips.
3. Dip the breadsticks in the egg mixture and place them in the two crisper plates.
4. Return the crisper plates to the Ninja Foodi Dual Zone Air Fryer.
5. Choose the Air Fry mode for Zone 1 and set the temperature to 390 degrees F and the time to 8 minutes.
6. Select the "MATCH" button to copy the settings for Zone 2.
7. Initiate cooking by pressing the START/STOP button.
8. Flip the French toast sticks when cooked halfway through.
9. Serve.

Nutrition Info:
- (Per serving) Calories 199 | Fat 11.1g |Sodium 297mg | Carbs 14.9g | Fiber 1g | Sugar 2.5g | Protein 9.9g

Bagels

Servings: 8
Cooking Time: 15 Minutes

Ingredients:
- 2 cups self-rising flour
- 2 cups non-fat plain Greek yogurt
- 2 beaten eggs for egg wash (optional)
- ½ cup sesame seeds (optional)

Directions:
1. In a medium mixing bowl, combine the self-rising flour and Greek yogurt using a wooden spoon.
2. Knead the dough for about 5 minutes on a lightly floured board.
3. Divide the dough into four equal pieces and roll each into a thin rope, securing the ends to form a bagel shape.
4. Install a crisper plate in both drawers. Place 4 bagels in a single layer in each drawer. Insert the drawers into the unit.
5. Select zone 1, select AIR FRY, set temperature to 360 degrees F/ 180 degrees C, and set time to 15 minutes. Select MATCH to match zone 2 settings to zone 1. Select START/STOP to begin.
6. Once the timer has finished, remove the bagels from the units.
7. Serve and enjoy!

Nutrition Info:
- (Per serving) Calories 202 | Fat 4.5g | Sodium 55mg | Carbs 31.3g | Fiber 2.7g | Sugar 4.7g | Protein 8.7g

Bacon And Egg Omelet

Servings:2
Cooking Time:10
Ingredients:
- 2 eggs, whisked
- ½ teaspoon of chopped tomatoes
- Sea Salt and black pepper, to taste
- 2 teaspoons of almond milk
- 1 teaspoon of cilantro, chopped
- 1 small green chili, chopped
- 4 slices of bacon

Directions:
1. Take a bowl and whisk eggs in it.
2. Then add green chili salt, black pepper, cilantro, almond milk, and chopped tomatoes.
3. Oil greases the ramekins.
4. Pour this into ramekins.
5. Put the bacon in the zone 1 basket and ramekins in zone 2 basket of the Ninja Foodie 2-Basket Air Fryer.
6. Now for zone 1, set it to AIR FRY mode at 400 degrees F for 10 minutes
7. And for zone 2, set it 350 degrees for 10 minutes in AIR FRY mode.
8. Press the Smart finish button and press start, it will finish both at the same time.
9. Once done, serve and enjoy.

Nutrition Info:
- (Per serving) Calories 285| Fat 21.5g| Sodium1000 mg | Carbs 2.2g | Fiber 0.1g| Sugar1 g | Protein 19.7g

Breakfast Casserole

Servings:4
Cooking Time:10
Ingredients:
- 1 pound of beef sausage, grounded
- 1/4 cup diced white onion
- 1 diced green bell pepper
- 8 whole eggs, beaten
- ½ cup Colby jack cheese, shredded
- ¼ teaspoon of garlic salt
- Oil spray, for greasing

Directions:
1. Take a bowl and add ground sausage to it.
2. Add in the diced onions, bell peppers, eggs and whisk it well.
3. Then season it with garlic salt.
4. Spray both the baskets of the air fryer with oil spray.
5. Divide this mixture among the baskets; remember to remove the crisper plates.
6. Top the mixture with cheese.
7. Now, turn ON the Ninja Foodie 2-Basket Air Fryer zone 1 and select AIR FRY mode and set the time to 10 minutes at 390 degrees F.
8. Select the MATCH button for zone 2 baskets, and hit start.
9. Once the cooking cycle completes, take out, and serve.
10. Serve and enjoy.

Nutrition Info:
- (Per serving) Calories 699| Fat 59.1g | Sodium 1217 mg | Carbs 6.8g | Fiber 0.6g| Sugar 2.5g | Protein33.1 g

Roasted Oranges

Servings: 4
Cooking Time: 6 Minutes

Ingredients:
- 2 oranges, halved
- 2 teaspoons honey
- 1 teaspoon cinnamon

Directions:
1. Place the oranges in each air fryer basket.
2. Drizzle honey and cinnamon over the orange halves.
3. Return the air fryer basket 1 to Zone 1, and basket 2 to Zone 2 of the Ninja Foodi 2-Basket Air Fryer.
4. Choose the "Air Fry" mode for Zone 1 at 395 degrees F temperature and 6 minutes of cooking time.
5. Select the "MATCH COOK" option to copy the settings for Zone 2.
6. Initiate cooking by pressing the START/PAUSE BUTTON.
7. Serve.

Nutrition Info:
- (Per serving) Calories 183 | Fat 15g |Sodium 402mg | Carbs 2.5g | Fiber 0.4g | Sugar 1.1g | Protein 10g

Blueberry Coffee Cake And Maple Sausage Patties

Servings:6
Cooking Time: 25 Minutes

Ingredients:
- FOR THE COFFEE CAKE
- 6 tablespoons unsalted butter, at room temperature, divided
- ⅓ cup granulated sugar
- 1 large egg
- 1 teaspoon vanilla extract
- ¼ cup whole milk
- 1½ cups all-purpose flour, divided
- 1 teaspoon baking powder
- ¼ teaspoon salt
- 1 cup blueberries
- ¼ cup packed light brown sugar
- ½ teaspoon ground cinnamon
- FOR THE SAUSAGE PATTIES
- ½ pound ground pork
- 2 tablespoons maple syrup
- ½ teaspoon dried sage
- ½ teaspoon dried thyme
- 1½ teaspoons kosher salt
- ½ teaspoon crushed fennel seeds
- ½ teaspoon red pepper flakes (optional)
- ¼ teaspoon freshly ground black pepper

Directions:
1. To prep the coffee cake: In a large bowl, cream together 4 tablespoons of butter with the granulated sugar. Beat in the egg, vanilla, and milk.
2. Stir in 1 cup of flour, along with the baking soda and salt, to form a thick batter. Fold in the blueberries.
3. In a second bowl, mix the remaining 2 tablespoons of butter, remaining ½ cup of flour, the brown sugar, and cinnamon to form a dry crumbly mixture.
4. To prep the sausage patties: In a large bowl, mix the pork, maple syrup, sage, thyme, salt, fennel seeds, red pepper flakes (if using), and black pepper until just combined.
5. Divide the mixture into 6 equal patties about ½ inch thick.
6. To cook the coffee cake and sausage patties: Spread the cake batter into the Zone 1 basket, top with the crumble mixture, and insert the basket in the unit. Install a crisper plate in the Zone 2 basket, add the sausage patties in a single layer, and insert the basket in the unit.
7. Select Zone 1, select BAKE, set the temperature to 350°F, and set the time to 25 minutes.
8. Select Zone 2, select AIR FRY, set the temperature to 375°F, and set the time to 12 minutes. Select SMART FINISH.
9. Press START/PAUSE to begin cooking.
10. When the Zone 2 timer reads 6 minutes, press START/PAUSE. Remove the basket and use silicone-tipped tongs to flip the sausage patties. Reinsert the basket and press START/PAUSE to resume cooking.
11. When cooking is complete, let the coffee cake cool for at least 5 minutes, then cut into 6 slices. Serve warm or at room temperature with the sausage patties.

Nutrition Info:
- (Per serving) Calories: 395; Total fat: 15g; Saturated fat: 8g; Carbohydrates: 53g; Fiber: 1.5g; Protein: 14g; Sodium: 187mg

Egg With Baby Spinach

Servings: 4
Cooking Time: 12

Ingredients:
- Nonstick spray, for greasing ramekins
- 2 tablespoons olive oil
- 6 ounces baby spinach
- 2 garlic cloves, minced
- 1/3 teaspoon kosher salt
- 6-8 large eggs
- ½ cup half and half
- Salt and black pepper, to taste
- 8 Sourdough bread slices, toasted

Directions:
1. Grease 4 ramekins with oil spray and set aside for further use.
2. Take a skillet and heat oil in it.
3. Then cook spinach for 2 minutes and add garlic and salt black pepper.
4. Let it simmer for 2 more minutes.
5. Once the spinach is wilted, transfer it to a plate.
6. Whisk an egg into a small bowl.
7. Add in the spinach.
8. Whisk it well and then pour half and half.
9. Divide this mixture between 4 ramekins and remember not to overfill it to the top, leave a little space on top.
10. Put the ramekins in zone 1 and zone 2 baskets of the Ninja Foodie 2-Basket Air Fryer.
11. Press start and set zone 1 to AIR fry it at 350 degrees F for 8-12 minutes.
12. Press the MATCH button for zone 2.
13. Once it's cooked and eggs are done, serve with sourdough bread slices.

Nutrition Info:
- (Per serving) Calories 404| Fat 19.6g| Sodium 761mg | Carbs 40.1g | Fiber 2.5g| Sugar 2.5g | Protein 19.2g

Spinach And Red Pepper Egg Cups With Coffee-glazed Canadian Bacon

Servings: 6
Cooking Time: 13 Minutes
Ingredients:
- FOR THE EGG CUPS
- 4 large eggs
- ¼ cup heavy (whipping) cream
- ¼ teaspoon kosher salt
- ¼ teaspoon freshly ground black pepper
- ½ cup roasted red peppers (about 1 whole pepper), drained and chopped
- ½ cup baby spinach, chopped
- FOR THE CANADIAN BACON
- ¼ cup brewed coffee
- 2 tablespoons maple syrup
- 1 tablespoon light brown sugar
- 6 slices Canadian bacon

Directions:
1. To prep the egg cups: In a medium bowl, whisk together the eggs and cream until well combined with a uniform, light color. Stir in the salt, black pepper, roasted red peppers, and spinach until combined.
2. Divide the egg mixture among 6 silicone muffin cups.
3. To prep the Canadian bacon: In a small bowl, whisk together the coffee, maple syrup, and brown sugar.
4. Using a basting brush, brush the glaze onto both sides of each slice of bacon.
5. To cook the egg cups and Canadian bacon: Install a crisper plate in each of the two baskets. Place the egg cups in the Zone 1 basket and insert the basket in the unit. Place the glazed bacon in the Zone 2 basket, making sure the slices don't overlap, and insert the basket in the unit. It is okay if the bacon overlaps a little bit.
6. Select Zone 1, select BAKE, set the temperature to 325°F, and set the time to 13 minutes.
7. Select Zone 2, select AIR FRY, set the temperature to 400°F, and set the time to 5 minutes. Select SMART FINISH.
8. Press START/PAUSE to begin cooking.
9. When the Zone 2 timer reads 2 minutes, press START/PAUSE. Remove the basket and use silicone-tipped tongs to flip the bacon. Reinsert the basket and press START/PAUSE to resume cooking.
10. When cooking is complete, serve the egg cups with the Canadian bacon.

Nutrition Info:
- (Per serving) Calories: 180; Total fat: 9.5g; Saturated fat: 4.5g; Carbohydrates: 9g; Fiber: 0g; Protein: 14g; Sodium: 688mg

Donuts

Servings: 6
Cooking Time: 15 Minutes
Ingredients:
- 1 cup granulated sugar
- 2 tablespoons ground cinnamon
- 1 can refrigerated flaky buttermilk biscuits
- ¼ cup unsalted butter, melted

Directions:
1. Combine the sugar and cinnamon in a small shallow bowl and set aside.
2. Remove the biscuits from the can and put them on a chopping board, separated. Cut holes in the center of each biscuit with a 1-inch round biscuit cutter (or a similarly sized bottle cap).
3. Place a crisper plate in each drawer. In each drawer, place 4 biscuits in a single layer. Insert the drawers into the unit.
4. Select zone 1, then AIR FRY, then set the temperature to 360 degrees F/ 180 degrees C with a 10-minute timer. To match zone 2 settings to zone 1, choose MATCH. To begin cooking, select START/STOP.
5. Remove the donuts from the drawers after the timer has finished.

Nutrition Info:
- (Per serving) Calories 223 | Fat 8g | Sodium 150mg | Carbs 40g | Fiber 1.4g | Sugar 34.2g | Protein 0.8g

Snacks And Appetizers Recipes

Cauliflower Cheese Patties

Servings: 4
Cooking Time: 10 Minutes

Ingredients:
- 2 eggs
- 200g cauliflower rice, microwave for 5 minutes
- 56g mozzarella cheese, shredded
- 22g parmesan cheese, grated
- 11g Mexican cheese, shredded
- ½ tsp onion powder
- 1 tsp dried basil
- 1 tsp garlic powder
- 33g breadcrumbs
- Pepper
- Salt

Directions:
1. Add cauliflower rice and remaining ingredients into the mixing bowl and mix until well combined.
2. Insert a crisper plate in the Ninja Foodi air fryer baskets.
3. Make patties from the cauliflower mixture and place them in both baskets.
4. Select zone 1, then select "air fry" mode and set the temperature to 390 degrees F for 10 minutes. Press "match" to match zone 2 settings to zone 1. Press "start/stop" to begin. Turn halfway through.

Nutrition Info:
- (Per serving) Calories 318 | Fat 18g |Sodium 951mg | Carbs 11.1g | Fiber 1.8g | Sugar 2.2g | Protein 25.6g

Chicken Tenders

Servings:3
Cooking Time:12

Ingredients:
- 1 pound of chicken tender
- Salt and black pepper, to taste
- 1 cup Panko bread crumbs
- 2 cups Italian bread crumbs
- 1 cup parmesan cheese
- 2 eggs
- Oil spray, for greasing

Directions:
1. Sprinkle the tenders with salt and black pepper.
2. In a medium bowl mix Panko bread crumbs with Italian breadcrumbs.
3. Add salt, pepper, and parmesan cheese.
4. Crack two eggs in a bowl.
5. First, put the chicken tender in eggs.
6. Now dredge the tender in a bowl and coat the tender well with crumbs.
7. Line both of the baskets of the air fryer with parchment paper.
8. At the end spray the tenders with oil spray.
9. Divided the tenders between the baskets of Ninja Foodie 2-Basket Air Fryer.
10. Set zone 1 basket to AIR FRY mode at 350 degrees F for 12 minutes.
11. Select the MATCH button for the zone 2 basket.
12. Once it's done, serve.

Nutrition Info:
- (Per serving) Calories558 | Fat23.8g | Sodium872 mg | Carbs 20.9g | Fiber1.7 g| Sugar2.2 g | Protein 63.5g

Parmesan French Fries

Servings: 6
Cooking Time: 20 Minutes.

Ingredients:
- 3 medium russet potatoes
- 2 tablespoons parmesan cheese
- 2 tablespoons fresh parsley, chopped
- 1 tablespoon olive oil
- Salt, to taste

Directions:
1. Wash the potatoes and pass them through the fries' cutter to get ¼-inch-thick fries.
2. Place the fries in a colander and drizzle salt on top.
3. Leave these fries for 10 minutes, then rinse.
4. Toss the potatoes with parmesan cheese, oil, salt, and parsley in a bowl.
5. Divide the potatoes into the two crisper plates.
6. Return the crisper plates to the Ninja Foodi Dual Zone Air Fryer.
7. Choose the Air Fry mode for Zone 1 and set the temperature to 360 degrees F and the time to 20 minutes.
8. Select the "MATCH" button to copy the settings for Zone 2.
9. Initiate cooking by pressing the START/STOP button.
10. Toss the chips once cooked halfway through, then resume cooking.
11. Serve warm.

Nutrition Info:
- (Per serving) Calories 307 | Fat 8.6g |Sodium 510mg | Carbs 22.2g | Fiber 1.4g | Sugar 13g | Protein 33.6g

Kale Potato Nuggets

Servings: 4
Cooking Time: 15minutes

Ingredients:
- 279g potatoes, chopped, boiled & mashed
- 268g kale, chopped
- 1 garlic clove, minced
- 30ml milk
- Pepper
- Salt

Directions:
1. In a bowl, mix potatoes, kale, milk, garlic, pepper, and salt until well combined.
2. Insert a crisper plate in the Ninja Foodi air fryer baskets.
3. Make small balls from the potato mixture and place them both baskets.
4. Select zone 1 then select "air fry" mode and set the temperature to 390 degrees F for 15 minutes. Press "match" to match zone 2 settings to zone 1. Press "start/stop" to begin. Turn halfway through.

Nutrition Info:
- (Per serving) Calories 90 | Fat 0.2g |Sodium 76mg | Carbs 19.4g | Fiber 2.8g | Sugar 1.2g | Protein 3.6g

Crispy Plantain Chips

Servings: 4
Cooking Time: 20 Minutes.

Ingredients:
- 1 green plantain
- 1 teaspoon canola oil
- ½ teaspoon sea salt

Directions:
1. Peel and cut the plantains into long strips using a mandolin slicer.
2. Grease the crisper plates with ½ teaspoon of canola oil.
3. Toss the plantains with salt and remaining canola oil.
4. Divide these plantains in the two crisper plates.
5. Return the crisper plate to the Ninja Foodi Dual Zone Air Fryer.
6. Choose the Air Fry mode for Zone 1 and set the temperature to 350 degrees F and the time to 20 minutes.
7. Select the "MATCH" button to copy the settings for Zone 2.
8. Initiate cooking by pressing the START/STOP button.
9. Toss the plantains after 10 minutes and resume cooking.
10. Serve warm.

Nutrition Info:
- (Per serving) Calories 122 | Fat 1.8g | Sodium 794mg | Carbs 17g | Fiber 8.9g | Sugar 1.6g | Protein 14.9g

Mac And Cheese Balls

Servings: 4
Cooking Time: 20 Minutes

Ingredients:
- 1 cup panko breadcrumbs
- 4 cups prepared macaroni and cheese, refrigerated
- 3 tablespoons flour
- 1 teaspoon salt, divided
- 1 teaspoon ground black pepper, divided
- 1 teaspoon smoked paprika, divided
- ½ teaspoon garlic powder, divided
- 2 eggs
- 1 tablespoon milk
- ¼ cup ranch dressing, garlic aioli, or chipotle mayo, for dipping (optional)

Directions:
1. Preheat a conventional oven to 400 degrees F/ 200 degrees C.
2. Shake the breadcrumbs onto a baking sheet so that they're evenly distributed. Bake in the oven for 3 minutes, then shake and bake for an additional 1 to 2 minutes, or until toasted.
3. Form the chilled macaroni and cheese into golf ball-sized balls and set them aside.
4. Combine the flour, ½ teaspoon salt, ½ teaspoon black pepper, ½ teaspoon smoked paprika, and ¼ teaspoon garlic powder in a large mixing bowl.
5. In a small bowl, whisk together the eggs and milk.
6. Combine the breadcrumbs, remaining salt, pepper, paprika, and garlic powder in a mixing bowl.
7. To coat the macaroni and cheese balls, roll them in the flour mixture, then the egg mixture, and then the breadcrumb mixture.
8. Place a crisper plate in each drawer. Put the cheese balls in a single layer in each drawer. Insert the drawers into the unit.
9. Select zone 1, then AIR FRY, then set the temperature to 360 degrees F/ 180 degrees C with an 8-minute timer. To match zone 2 settings to zone 1, choose MATCH. To begin, select START/STOP.
10. Serve and enjoy!

Nutrition Info:
- (Per serving) Calories 489 | Fat 15.9g | Sodium 1402mg | Carbs 69.7g | Fiber 2.5g | Sugar 4g | Protein 16.9g

Onion Rings

Servings: 4
Cooking Time: 7 Minutes

Ingredients:
- 170g onion, sliced into rings
- ½ cup breadcrumbs
- 2 eggs, beaten
- ½ cup flour
- Salt and black pepper to taste

Directions:
1. Mix flour, black pepper and salt in a bowl.
2. Dredge the onion rings through the flour mixture.
3. Dip them in the eggs and coat with the breadcrumbs.
4. Place the coated onion rings in the air fryer baskets.
5. Return the air fryer basket 1 to Zone 1, and basket 2 to Zone 2 of the Ninja Foodi 2-Basket Air Fryer.
6. Choose the "Air Fry" mode for Zone 1 at 350 degrees F and 7 minutes of cooking time.
7. Select the "MATCH COOK" option to copy the settings for Zone 2.
8. Initiate cooking by pressing the START/PAUSE BUTTON.
9. Shake the rings once cooked halfway through.
10. Serve warm.

Nutrition Info:
- (Per serving) Calories 185 | Fat 11g |Sodium 355mg | Carbs 21g | Fiber 5.8g | Sugar 3g | Protein 4.7g

Dried Apple Chips Dried Banana Chips

Servings:6
Cooking Time: 6 To 10 Hours

Ingredients:
- FOR THE APPLE CHIPS
- ½ teaspoon ground cinnamon
- ¼ teaspoon ground nutmeg
- ⅛ teaspoon ground allspice
- ⅛ teaspoon ground ginger
- 2 Gala apples, cored and cut into ⅛-inch-thick rings
- FOR THE BANANA CHIPS
- 2 firm-ripe bananas, cut into ¼-inch slices

Directions:
1. To prep the apple chips: In a small bowl, mix the cinnamon, nutmeg, allspice, and ginger until combined. Sprinkle the spice mixture over the apple slices.
2. To dehydrate the fruit: Arrange half of the apple slices in a single layer in the Zone 1 basket. It is okay if the edges overlap a bit as they will shrink as they cook. Place a crisper plate on top of the apples. Arrange the remaining apple slices on top of the crisper plate and insert the basket in the unit.
3. Repeat this process with the bananas in the Zone 2 basket and insert the basket in the unit.
4. Select Zone 1, select DEHYDRATE, set the temperature to 135°F, and set the time to 8 hours.
5. Select Zone 2, select DEHYDRATE, set the temperature to 135°F, and set the time to 10 hours. Select SMART FINISH.
6. Press START/PAUSE to begin cooking.
7. When both timers read 2 hours, press START/PAUSE. Remove both baskets and check the fruit for doneness; note that juicier fruit will take longer to dry than fruit that starts out drier. Reinsert the basket and press START/PAUSE to continue cooking if necessary.

Nutrition Info:
- (Per serving) Calories: 67; Total fat: 0g; Saturated fat: 0g; Carbohydrates: 16g; Fiber: 3g; Protein: 0g; Sodium: 1mg

Cinnamon Sugar Chickpeas

Servings: 4
Cooking Time: 15 Minutes
Ingredients:
- 2 cups chickpeas, drained
- Spray oil
- 1 tablespoon coconut sugar
- ½ teaspoon cinnamon
- Serving
- 57g cheddar cheese, cubed
- ¼ cup raw almonds
- 85g jerky, sliced

Directions:
1. Toss chickpeas with coconut sugar, cinnamon and oil in a bowl.
2. Divide the chickpeas into the Ninja Foodi 2 Baskets Air Fryer baskets.
3. Drizzle cheddar cheese, almonds and jerky on top.
4. Return the air fryer basket 1 to Zone 1, and basket 2 to Zone 2 of the Ninja Foodi 2-Basket Air Fryer.
5. Choose the "Air Fry" mode for Zone 1 at 380 degrees F and 15 minutes of cooking time.
6. Select the "MATCH COOK" option to copy the settings for Zone 2.
7. Initiate cooking by pressing the START/PAUSE BUTTON.
8. Toss the chickpeas once cooked halfway through.
9. Serve warm.

Nutrition Info:
- (Per serving) Calories 103 | Fat 8.4g |Sodium 117mg | Carbs 3.5g | Fiber 0.9g | Sugar 1.5g | Protein 5.1g

Bacon Wrapped Tater Tots

Servings: 8
Cooking Time: 14 Minutes
Ingredients:
- 8 bacon slices
- 3 tablespoons honey
- ½ tablespoon chipotle chile powder
- 16 frozen tater tots

Directions:
1. Cut the bacon slices in half and wrap each tater tot with a bacon slice.
2. Brush the bacon with honey and drizzle chipotle chile powder over them.
3. Insert a toothpick to seal the bacon.
4. Place the wrapped tots in the air fryer baskets.
5. Return the air fryer basket 1 to Zone 1, and basket 2 to Zone 2 of the Ninja Foodi 2-Basket Air Fryer.
6. Choose the "Air Fry" mode for Zone 1 at 350 degrees F and 14 minutes of cooking time.
7. Select the "MATCH COOK" option to copy the settings for Zone 2.
8. Initiate cooking by pressing the START/PAUSE BUTTON.
9. Serve warm.

Nutrition Info:
- (Per serving) Calories 100 | Fat 2g |Sodium 480mg | Carbs 4g | Fiber 2g | Sugar 0g | Protein 18g

Crispy Chickpeas

Servings: 4
Cooking Time: 15 Minutes
Ingredients:
- 1 (15-ounce) can unsalted chickpeas, rinsed and drained
- 1½ tablespoons toasted sesame oil
- ¼ teaspoon smoked paprika
- ¼ teaspoon crushed red pepper
- ⅛ teaspoon salt
- Cooking spray
- 2 lime wedges

Directions:
1. The chickpeas should be spread out over multiple layers of paper towels. Roll the chickpeas under the paper towels to dry both sides, then top with more paper towels and pat until completely dry.
2. In a medium mixing bowl, combine the chickpeas and oil. Add the paprika, crushed red pepper, and salt to taste.
3. Place a crisper plate in each drawer. Put the chickpeas in a single layer in each drawer. Insert the drawers into the unit.
4. Select zone 1, then ROAST, then set the temperature to 400 degrees F/ 200 degrees C with a 15-minute timer. To match zone 2 settings to zone 1, choose MATCH. To begin, select START/STOP.

Nutrition Info:
- (Per serving) Calories 169 | Fat 5g | Sodium 357mg | Carbs 27.3g | Fiber 5.7g | Sugar 0.6g | Protein 5.9g

Grill Cheese Sandwich

Servings: 2
Cooking Time: 10
Ingredients:
- 4 slices of white bread slices
- 2 tablespoons of butter, melted
- 2 slices of sharp cheddar
- 2 slices of Swiss cheese
- 2 slices of mozzarella cheese

Directions:
1. Brush melted butter on one side of all the bread slices and then top the 2 bread slices with slices of cheddar, Swiss, and mozzarella, one slice per bread.
2. Top it with the other slice to make a sandwich.
3. Divide it between two baskets of the air fryer.
4. Turn on AIR FRY mode for zone 1 basket at 350 degrees F for 10 minutes.
5. Use the MATCH button for the second zone.
6. Once done, serve.

Nutrition Info:
- (Per serving) Calories 577 | Fat 38g | Sodium 1466mg | Carbs 30.5g | Fiber 1.1g| Sugar 6.5g | Protein 27.6g

Chili-lime Crispy Chickpeas Pizza-seasoned Crispy Chickpeas

Servings: 6
Cooking Time: 20 Minutes

Ingredients:

- FOR THE CHILI-LIME CHICKPEAS
- 1½ cups canned chickpeas, rinsed and drained
- ¼ cup fresh lime juice
- 1 tablespoon olive oil
- 1½ teaspoons chili powder
- ½ teaspoon kosher salt
- FOR THE PIZZA-SEASONED CHICKPEAS
- 1½ cups canned chickpeas, rinsed and drained
- 1 tablespoon olive oil
- 1 tablespoon grated Parmesan cheese
- ½ teaspoon dried basil
- ½ teaspoon dried oregano
- ½ teaspoon kosher salt
- ¼ teaspoon onion powder
- ¼ teaspoon garlic powder
- ¼ teaspoon fennel seeds
- ¼ teaspoon dried thyme
- ¼ teaspoon red pepper flakes (optional)

Directions:

1. To prep the chili-lime chickpeas: In a small bowl, mix the chickpeas, lime juice, olive oil, chili powder, and salt until the chickpeas are well coated.
2. To prep the pizza-seasoned chickpeas: In a small bowl, mix the chickpeas, olive oil, Parmesan, basil, oregano, salt, onion powder, garlic powder, fennel, thyme, and red pepper flakes (if using) until the chickpeas are well coated.
3. To cook the chickpeas: Install a crisper plate in each of the two baskets. Place the chili-lime chickpeas in the Zone 1 basket and insert the basket in the unit. Place the pizza-seasoned chickpeas in the Zone 2 basket and insert the basket in the unit.
4. Select Zone 1, select AIR FRY, set the temperature to 375°F, and set the time to 20 minutes. Select MATCH COOK to match Zone 2 settings to Zone 1.
5. Press START/PAUSE to begin cooking.
6. When both timers read 10 minutes, press START/PAUSE. Remove both baskets and give each basket a shake to redistribute the chickpeas. Reinsert both baskets and press START/PAUSE to resume cooking.
7. When both timers read 5 minutes, press START/PAUSE. Remove both baskets and give each basket a good shake again. Reinsert both baskets and press START/PAUSE to resume cooking.
8. When cooking is complete, the chickpeas will be crisp and golden brown. Serve warm or at room temperature.

Nutrition Info:

- (Per serving) Calories: 145; Total fat: 6.5g; Saturated fat: 0.5g; Carbohydrates: 17g; Fiber: 4.5g; Protein: 5g; Sodium: 348mg

Tater Tots

Servings: 4
Cooking Time: 8 Minutes

Ingredients:

- 16 ounces tater tots
- ½ cup shredded cheddar cheese
- 1½ teaspoons bacon bits
- 2 green onions, chopped
- Sour cream (optional)

Directions:

1. Place a crisper plate in each drawer. Put the tater tots into the drawers in a single layer. Insert the drawers into the unit.
2. Select zone 1, then AIR FRY, then set the temperature to 360 degrees F/ 180 degrees C with a 6-minute timer. To match zone 2 settings to zone 1, choose MATCH. To begin, select START/STOP.
3. When the cooking time is over, add the shredded cheddar cheese, bacon bits, and green onions over the tater tots. Select zone 1, AIR FRY, 360 degrees F/ 180 degrees C, for 4 minutes. Select MATCH. Press START/STOP.
4. Drizzle sour cream over the top before serving.
5. Enjoy!

Nutrition Info:

- (Per serving) Calories 335 | Fat 19.1g | Sodium 761mg | Carbs 34.1g | Fiber 3g | Sugar 0.6g | Protein 8.9g

Crab Cakes

Servings: 4
Cooking Time: 10 Minutes
Ingredients:
- 227g lump crab meat
- 1 red capsicum, chopped
- 3 green onions, chopped
- 3 tablespoons mayonnaise
- 3 tablespoons breadcrumbs
- 2 teaspoons old bay seasoning
- 1 teaspoon lemon juice

Directions:
1. Mix crab meat with capsicum, onions and the rest of the ingredients in a food processor.
2. Make 4 inch crab cakes out of this mixture.
3. Divide the crab cakes into the Ninja Foodi 2 Baskets Air Fryer baskets.
4. Return the air fryer basket 1 to Zone 1, and basket 2 to Zone 2 of the Ninja Foodi 2-Basket Air Fryer.
5. Choose the "Air Fry" mode for Zone 1 at 370 degrees F and 10 minutes of cooking time.
6. Select the "MATCH COOK" option to copy the settings for Zone 2.
7. Initiate cooking by pressing the START/PAUSE BUTTON.
8. Flip the crab cakes once cooked halfway through.
9. Serve warm.

Nutrition Info:
- (Per serving) Calories 163 | Fat 11.5g |Sodium 918mg | Carbs 8.3g | Fiber 4.2g | Sugar 0.2g | Protein 7.4g

Parmesan Crush Chicken

Servings:4
Cooking Time:18
Ingredients:
- 4 chicken breasts
- 1 cup parmesan cheese
- 1 cup bread crumb
- 2 eggs, whisked
- Salt, to taste
- Oil spray, for greasing

Directions:
1. Whisk egg in a large bowl and set aside.
2. Season the chicken breast with salt and then put it in egg wash.
3. Next, dredge it in breadcrumb then parmesan cheese.
4. Line both the basket of the air fryer with parchment paper.
5. Divided the breast pieces between the backsets, and oil spray the breast pieces.
6. Set zone 1 basket to air fry mode at 350 degrees F for 18 minutes.
7. Select the MATCH button for the zone 2 basket.
8. Once it's done, serve.

Nutrition Info:
- (Per serving) Calories574 | Fat25g | Sodium848 mg | Carbs 21.4g | Fiber 1.2g| Sugar 1.8g | Protein 64.4g

Stuffed Bell Peppers

Servings: 3
Cooking Time: 16

Ingredients:

- 6 large bell peppers
- 1-1/2 cup cooked rice
- 2 cups cheddar cheese

Directions:

1. Cut the bell peppers in half lengthwise and remove all the seeds.
2. Fill the cavity of each bell pepper with cooked rice.
3. Divide the bell peppers amongst the two zones of the air fryer basket.
4. Set the time for zone 1 for 200 degrees for 10 minutes.
5. Select MATCH button of zone 2 basket.
6. Afterward, take out the baskets and sprinkle cheese on top.
7. Set the time for zone 1 for 200 degrees for 6 minutes.
8. Select MATCH button of zone 2 basket.
9. Once it's done, serve.

Nutrition Info:

- (Per serving) Calories 605| Fat 26g | Sodium477 mg | Carbs68.3 g | Fiber4 g| Sugar 12.5g | Protein25.6 g

Tofu Veggie Meatballs

Servings: 4
Cooking Time: 10minutes

Ingredients:

- 122g firm tofu, drained
- 50g breadcrumbs
- 37g bamboo shoots, thinly sliced
- 22g carrots, shredded & steamed
- 1 tsp garlic powder
- 1 ½ tbsp soy sauce
- 2 tbsp cornstarch
- 3 dried shitake mushrooms, soaked & chopped
- Pepper
- Salt

Directions:

1. Add tofu and remaining ingredients into the food processor and process until well combined.
2. Insert a crisper plate in the Ninja Foodi air fryer baskets.
3. Make small balls from the tofu mixture and place them in both baskets.
4. Select zone 1, then select "air fry" mode and set the temperature to 380 degrees F for 10 minutes. Press "match" to match zone 2 settings to zone 1. Press "start/stop" to begin. Turn halfway through.

Nutrition Info:

- (Per serving) Calories 125 | Fat 1.8g |Sodium 614mg | Carbs 23.4g | Fiber 2.5g | Sugar 3.8g | Protein 5.3g

Jalapeño Popper Chicken

Servings: 4
Cooking Time: 50 Minutes
Ingredients:
- 2 ounces cream cheese, softened
- ¼ cup shredded cheddar cheese
- ¼ cup shredded mozzarella cheese
- ¼ teaspoon garlic powder
- 4 small jalapeño peppers, seeds removed and diced
- Kosher salt, as desired
- Ground black pepper, as desired
- 4 organic boneless, skinless chicken breasts
- 8 slices bacon

Directions:
1. Cream together the cream cheese, cheddar cheese, mozzarella cheese, garlic powder, and jalapeño in a mixing bowl. Add salt and pepper to taste.
2. Make a deep pocket in the center of each chicken breast, but be cautious not to cut all the way through.
3. Fill each chicken breast's pocket with the cream cheese mixture.
4. Wrap two strips of bacon around each chicken breast and attach them with toothpicks.
5. Place a crisper plate in each drawer. Put the chicken breasts in the drawers. Place both drawers in the unit.
6. Select zone 1, then AIR FRY, and set the temperature to 350 degrees F/ 175 degrees C with a 30-minute timer. To match zone 2 and zone 1 settings, select MATCH. To begin cooking, press the START/STOP button.
7. When cooking is complete, remove the chicken breasts and allow them to rest for 5 minutes before serving

Nutrition Info:
- (Per serving) Calories 507 | Fat 27.5g | Sodium 1432mg | Carbs 2.3g | Fiber 0.6g | Sugar 0.6g | Protein 58.2g

Crab Rangoon Dip With Crispy Wonton Strips

Servings:6
Cooking Time: 15 Minutes
Ingredients:
- FOR THE DIP
- 1 (6-ounce) can pink crab, drained
- 8 ounces (16 tablespoons) cream cheese, at room temperature
- ½ cup sour cream
- 1 tablespoon chopped scallions
- ½ teaspoon garlic powder
- 1 teaspoon Worcestershire sauce
- ¼ teaspoon kosher salt
- 1 cup shredded part-skim mozzarella cheese
- FOR THE WONTON STRIPS
- 12 wonton wrappers
- 1 tablespoon olive oil
- ¼ teaspoon kosher salt

Directions:
1. To prep the dip: In a medium bowl, mix the crab, cream cheese, sour cream, scallions, garlic powder, Worcestershire sauce, and salt until smooth.
2. To prep the wonton strips: Brush both sides of the wonton wrappers with the oil and sprinkle with salt. Cut the wonton wrappers into ¾-inch-wide strips.
3. To cook the dip and strips: Pour the dip into the Zone 1 basket, top with the mozzarella cheese, and insert the basket in the unit. Install a crisper plate in the Zone 2 basket, add the wonton strips, and insert the basket in the unit.
4. Select Zone 1, select BAKE, set the temperature to 330°F, and set the time to 15 minutes.
5. Select Zone 2, select AIR FRY, set the temperature to 350°F, and set the time to 6 minutes. Select SMART FINISH.
6. Press START/PAUSE to begin cooking.
7. When the Zone 2 timer reads 4 minutes, press START/PAUSE. Remove the basket and shake well to redistribute the wonton strips. Reinsert the basket and press START/PAUSE to resume cooking.
8. When the Zone 2 timer reads 2 minutes, press START/PAUSE. Remove the basket and shake well to redistribute the wonton strips. Reinsert the basket and press START/PAUSE to resume cooking.
9. When cooking is complete, the dip will be bubbling and golden brown on top and the wonton strips will be crunchy. Serve warm.

Nutrition Info:
- (Per serving) Calories: 315; Total fat: 23g; Saturated fat: 12g; Carbohydrates: 14g; Fiber: 0.5g; Protein: 14g; Sodium: 580mg

Avocado Fries With Sriracha Dip

Servings: 4
Cooking Time: 6 Minutes
Ingredients:
- Avocado Fries
- 4 avocados, peeled and cut into sticks
- ¾ cup panko breadcrumbs
- ¼ cup flour
- 2 eggs, beaten
- ½ teaspoon garlic powder
- ½ teaspoon salt
- SRIRACHA-RANCH SAUCE
- ¼ cup ranch dressing
- 1 teaspoon sriracha sauce

Directions:
1. Mix flour with garlic powder and salt in a bowl.
2. Dredge the avocado sticks through the flour mixture.
3. Dip them in the eggs and coat them with breadcrumbs.
4. Place the coated fries in the air fryer baskets.
5. Return the air fryer basket 1 to Zone 1, and basket 2 to Zone 2 of the Ninja Foodi 2-Basket Air Fryer.
6. Choose the "Air Fry" mode for Zone 1 at 400 degrees F and 6 minutes of cooking time.
7. Select the "MATCH COOK" option to copy the settings for Zone 2.
8. Initiate cooking by pressing the START/PAUSE BUTTON.
9. Flip the fries once cooked halfway through.
10. Mix all the dipping sauce ingredients in a bowl.
11. Serve the fries with dipping sauce.

Nutrition Info:
- (Per serving) Calories 229 | Fat 1.9 |Sodium 567mg | Carbs 1.9g | Fiber 0.4g | Sugar 0.6g | Protein 11.8g

Crab Cake Poppers

Servings: 6
Cooking Time: 10 Minutes
Ingredients:
- 1 egg, lightly beaten
- 453g lump crab meat, drained
- 1 tsp garlic, minced
- 1 tsp lemon juice
- 1 tsp old bay seasoning
- 30g almond flour
- 1 tsp Dijon mustard
- 28g mayonnaise
- Pepper
- Salt

Directions:
1. In a bowl, mix crab meat and remaining ingredients until well combined.
2. Make small balls from the crab meat mixture and place them on a plate.
3. Place the plate in the refrigerator for 50 minutes.
4. Insert a crisper plate in the Ninja Foodi air fryer baskets.
5. Place the prepared crab meatballs in both baskets.
6. Select zone 1 then select "air fry" mode and set the temperature to 360 degrees F for 10 minutes. Press "match" to match zone 2 settings to zone 1. Press "start/stop" to begin.

Nutrition Info:
- (Per serving) Calories 86 | Fat 8.5g |Sodium 615mg | Carbs 2.7g | Fiber 0.1g | Sugar 0.4g | Protein 12g

Jalapeño Popper Dip With Tortilla Chips

Servings: 6
Cooking Time: 15 Minutes
Ingredients:
- FOR THE DIP
- 8 ounces cream cheese, at room temperature
- ½ cup sour cream
- 1 cup shredded Cheddar cheese
- ¼ cup shredded Parmesan cheese
- ¼ cup roughly chopped pickled jalapeños
- ½ teaspoon kosher salt
- ½ cup panko bread crumbs
- 2 tablespoons olive oil
- ½ teaspoon dried parsley
- FOR THE TORTILLA CHIPS
- 10 corn tortillas
- 2 tablespoons fresh lime juice
- 1 tablespoon olive oil
- ½ teaspoon kosher salt

Directions:
1. To prep the dip: In a medium bowl, mix the cream cheese, sour cream, Cheddar, Parmesan, jalapeños, and salt until smooth.
2. In a small bowl, combine the panko, olive oil, and parsley.
3. Pour the dip into a 14-ounce ramekin and top with the panko mixture.
4. To prep the chips: Brush both sides of each tortilla with lime juice, then with oil. Sprinkle with the salt. Using a sharp knife or a pizza cutter, cut each tortilla into 4 wedges.
5. To cook the dip and chips: Install a crisper plate in each of the two baskets. Place the ramekin of dip in the Zone 1 basket and insert the basket in the unit. Layer the tortillas in the Zone 2 basket and insert the basket in the unit.
6. Select Zone 1, select BAKE, set the temperature to 350°F, and set the time to 15 minutes.
7. Select Zone 2, select AIR FRY, set the temperature to 375°F, and set the time to 5 minutes. Select SMART FINISH.
8. Press START/PAUSE to begin cooking.
9. When the Zone 2 timer reads 3 minutes, press START/PAUSE. Remove the basket from the unit and give the basket a good shake to redistribute the chips. Reinsert the basket and press START/PAUSE to resume cooking.
10. When cooking is complete, the dip will be bubbling and golden brown and the chips will be crispy. Serve warm.

Nutrition Info:
- (Per serving) Calories: 406; Total fat: 31g; Saturated fat: 14g; Carbohydrates: 22g; Fiber: 1g; Protein: 11g; Sodium: 539mg

Mozzarella Balls

Servings: 6
Cooking Time: 13 Minutes
Ingredients:
- 2 cups mozzarella, shredded
- 3 tablespoons cornstarch
- 3 tablespoons water
- 2 eggs, beaten
- 1 cup Italian seasoned breadcrumbs
- 1 tablespoon Italian seasoning
- 1½ teaspoons garlic powder
- 1 teaspoon salt
- 1½ teaspoons Parmesan

Directions:
1. Mix mozzarella with parmesan, water and cornstarch in a bowl.
2. Make 1-inch balls out of this mixture.
3. Mix breadcrumbs with seasoning, salt, and garlic powder in a bowl.
4. Dip the balls into the beaten eggs and coat with the breadcrumbs.
5. Place the coated balls in the air fryer baskets.
6. Return the air fryer basket 1 to Zone 1, and basket 2 to Zone 2 of the Ninja Foodi 2-Basket Air Fryer.
7. Choose the "Air Fry" mode for Zone 1 and set the temperature to 360 degrees F and 13 minutes of cooking time.
8. Select the "MATCH COOK" option to copy the settings for Zone 2.
9. Initiate cooking by pressing the START/PAUSE BUTTON.
10. Toss the balls once cooked halfway through.
11. Serve.

Nutrition Info:
- (Per serving) Calories 307 | Fat 8.6g | Sodium 510mg | Carbs 22.2g | Fiber 1.4g | Sugar 13g | Protein 33.6g

Beef, Pork, And Lamb Recipes

Lamb Shank With Mushroom Sauce

Servings: 4
Cooking Time: 35 Minutes.
Ingredients:
- 20 mushrooms, chopped
- 2 red bell pepper, chopped
- 2 red onion, chopped
- 1 cup red wine
- 4 leeks, chopped
- 6 tablespoons balsamic vinegar
- 2 teaspoons black pepper
- 2 teaspoons salt
- 3 tablespoons fresh rosemary
- 6 garlic cloves
- 4 lamb shanks
- 3 tablespoons olive oil

Directions:
1. Season the lamb shanks with salt, pepper, rosemary, and 1 teaspoon of olive oil.
2. Set half of the shanks in each of the crisper plate.
3. Return the crisper plate to the Ninja Foodi Dual Zone Air Fryer.
4. Choose the Air Fry mode for Zone 1 and set the temperature to 390 degrees F and the time to 25 minutes.
5. Select the "MATCH" button to copy the settings for Zone 2.
6. Initiate cooking by pressing the START/STOP button.
7. Flip the shanks halfway through, and resume cooking.
8. Meanwhile, add and heat the remaining olive oil in a skillet.
9. Add onion and garlic to sauté for 5 minutes.
10. Add in mushrooms and cook for 5 minutes.
11. Add red wine and cook until it is absorbed
12. Stir all the remaining vegetables along with black pepper and salt.
13. Cook until vegetables are al dente.
14. Serve the air fried shanks with sautéed vegetable fry.

Nutrition Info:
- (Per serving) Calories 352 | Fat 9.1g |Sodium 1294mg | Carbs 3.9g | Fiber 1g | Sugar 1g | Protein 61g

Pork Tenderloin With Brown Sugar–pecan Sweet Potatoes

Servings:4
Cooking Time: 45 Minutes
Ingredients:
- FOR THE PORK TENDERLOIN
- 1½ pounds pork tenderloin
- 2 teaspoons vegetable oil
- ½ teaspoon kosher salt
- ½ teaspoon poultry seasoning
- FOR THE SWEET POTATOES
- 4 teaspoons unsalted butter, at room temperature
- 2 tablespoons dark brown sugar
- ¼ cup chopped pecans
- 4 small sweet potatoes

Directions:
1. To prep the pork: Coat the pork tenderloin with the oil, then rub with the salt and poultry seasoning.
2. To prep the sweet potatoes: In a small bowl, mix the butter, brown sugar, and pecans until well combined.
3. To cook the pork and sweet potatoes: Install a crisper plate in the Zone 1 basket. Place the pork tenderloin in the basket and insert the basket in the unit. Place the sweet potatoes in the Zone 2 basket and insert the basket in the unit.
4. Select Zone 1, select AIR FRY, set the temperature to 390°F, and set the time to 25 minutes.
5. Select Zone 2, select BAKE, set the temperature to 400°F, and set the time to 45 minutes. Select SMART FINISH.
6. Press START/PAUSE to begin cooking.
7. When the Zone 2 timer reads 10 minutes, press START/PAUSE. Remove the basket. Slice the sweet potatoes open lengthwise. Divide the pecan mixture among the potatoes. Reinsert the basket and press START/PAUSE to resume cooking.
8. When cooking is complete, the pork will be cooked through (an instant-read thermometer should read 145°F) and the potatoes will be soft and their flesh fluffy.
9. Transfer the pork loin to a plate or cutting board and let rest for at least 5 minutes before slicing and serving.

Nutrition Info:
- (Per serving) Calories: 415; Total fat: 15g; Saturated fat: 4.5g; Carbohydrates: 33g; Fiber: 4.5g; Protein: 36g; Sodium: 284mg

Pork Chops And Potatoes

Servings: 3
Cooking Time: 12 Minutes
Ingredients:
- 455g red potatoes
- Olive oil
- Salt and pepper
- 1 teaspoon garlic powder
- 1 teaspoon fresh rosemary, chopped
- 2 tablespoons brown sugar
- 1 tablespoon soy sauce
- 1 tablespoon Worcestershire sauce
- 1 teaspoon lemon juice
- 3 small pork chops

Directions:
1. Mix potatoes and pork chops with remaining ingredients in a bowl.
2. Divide the ingredients in the air fryer baskets.
3. Return the air fryer basket 1 to Zone 1, and basket 2 to Zone 2 of the Ninja Foodi 2-Basket Air Fryer.
4. Choose the "Air Fry" mode for Zone 1 at 400 degrees F and 12 minutes of cooking time.
5. Select the "MATCH COOK" option to copy the settings for Zone 2.
6. Initiate cooking by pressing the START/PAUSE BUTTON.
7. Flip the chops and toss potatoes once cooked halfway through.
8. Serve warm.

Nutrition Info:
- (Per serving) Calories 352 | Fat 9.1g |Sodium 1294mg | Carbs 3.9g | Fiber 1g | Sugar 1g | Protein 61g

Pork Chops With Apples

Servings: 2
Cooking Time: 15 Minutes
Ingredients:
- ½ small red cabbage, sliced
- 1 apple, sliced
- 1 sweet onion, sliced
- 2 tablespoons oil
- ½ teaspoon cumin
- ½ teaspoon paprika
- Salt and black pepper, to taste
- 2 boneless pork chops (1″ thick)

Directions:
1. Toss pork chops with apple and the rest of the ingredients in a bowl.
2. Divide the mixture in the air fryer baskets.
3. Return the air fryer basket 1 to Zone 1, and basket 2 to Zone 2 of the Ninja Foodi 2-Basket Air Fryer.
4. Choose the "Air Fry" mode for Zone 1 and set the temperature to 400 degrees F and 15 minutes of cooking time.
5. Select the "MATCH COOK" option to copy the settings for Zone 2.
6. Initiate cooking by pressing the START/PAUSE BUTTON.
7. Serve warm.

Nutrition Info:
- (Per serving) Calories 374 | Fat 25g |Sodium 275mg | Carbs 7.3g | Fiber 0g | Sugar 6g | Protein 12.3g

Cilantro Lime Steak

Servings: 4
Cooking Time: 10 Minutes
Ingredients:
- 450g flank steak, sliced
- 1 tsp cumin
- 1 tsp olive oil
- 4 tsp soy sauce
- 12g cilantro, chopped
- ¼ tsp cayenne
- 45ml lime juice
- 2 tsp chilli powder
- ¼ tsp salt

Directions:
1. Add the sliced steak pieces and the remaining ingredients into a zip-lock bag. Seal the bag and place in the refrigerator for 2 hours.
2. Insert a crisper plate in the Ninja Foodi air fryer baskets.
3. Place the marinated steak pieces in both baskets.
4. Select zone 1, then select "air fry" mode and set the temperature to 380 degrees F for 10 minutes. Press "match" to match zone 2 settings to zone 1. Press "start/stop" to begin.

Nutrition Info:
- (Per serving) Calories 240 | Fat 11g | Sodium 524mg | Carbs 1.5g | Fiber 0.6g | Sugar 0.2g | Protein 32.2g

Marinated Pork Chops

Servings: 2
Cooking Time: 12 Minutes
Ingredients:
- 2 pork chops, boneless
- 18g sugar
- 1 tbsp water
- 15ml rice wine
- 15ml dark soy sauce
- 15ml light soy sauce
- ½ tsp cinnamon
- ½ tsp five-spice powder
- 1 tsp black pepper

Directions:
1. Add pork chops and remaining ingredients into a zip-lock bag. Seal the bag and place in the refrigerator for 4 hours.
2. Insert a crisper plate in the Ninja Foodi air fryer baskets.
3. Place the marinated pork chops in both baskets.
4. Select zone 1, then select air fry mode and set the temperature to 380 degrees F for 12 minutes. Press "match" to match zone 2 settings to zone 1. Press "start/stop" to begin.

Nutrition Info:
- (Per serving) Calories 306 | Fat 19.9g | Sodium 122mg | Carbs 13.7g | Fiber 0.6g | Sugar 11g | Protein 18.1g

Strip Steaks With Hasselback Potatoes

Servings: 4
Cooking Time: 30 Minutes
Ingredients:
- FOR THE STRIP STEAK
- 2 boneless strip steaks (8 ounces each)
- 2 teaspoons vegetable oil
- 1 tablespoon steak seasoning
- FOR THE HASSELBACK POTATOES
- 4 russet potatoes
- 1 tablespoon vegetable oil
- 1 teaspoon kosher salt
- 1 tablespoon salted butter, at room temperature
- 2 teaspoons minced garlic
- 2 teaspoons minced fresh parsley

Directions:
1. To prep the strip steak: Brush both sides of the steaks with the oil and season with the steak seasoning.
2. To prep the Hasselback potatoes: Set a potato on a work surface and lay the handles of two wooden spoons lengthwise on either side of the potato. Make crosswise slits along the potato, spacing them ⅛ inch apart, being careful to not cut the potato completely through (the spoon handles will prevent you from cutting all the way through). Repeat with the remaining potatoes.
3. Rub the potatoes with the oil and season with salt.
4. In a small bowl, mix the butter, garlic, and parsley until smooth.
5. To cook the steak and potatoes: Install a crisper plate in each of the two baskets. Place the steaks in the Zone 1 basket and insert the basket in the unit. Place the potatoes in the Zone 2 basket and insert the basket in the unit.
6. Select Zone 1, select AIR FRY, set the temperature to 375°F, and set the time to 20 minutes.
7. Select Zone 2, select BAKE, set the temperature to 375°F, and set the time to 30 minutes. Select SMART FINISH.
8. Press START/PAUSE to begin cooking.
9. When both timers read 6 minutes, press START/PAUSE. Remove the Zone 1 basket and use silicone-tipped tongs to flip the steaks. Reinsert the basket in the unit. Remove the Zone 2 basket and spread the herb butter into the potatoes, being sure to work the butter in between the slices. Reinsert the basket and press START/PAUSE to resume cooking.
10. When cooking is complete, the steak should be cooked to your liking and the potato soft when pierced with a fork.
11. Remove the steaks from the basket and let rest for 5 minutes before slicing.

Nutrition Info:
- (Per serving) Calories: 361; Total fat: 15g; Saturated fat: 5g; Carbohydrates: 31g; Fiber: 2g; Protein: 25g; Sodium: 694mg

Beef Ribs I

Servings: 2
Cooking Time: 15
Ingredients:
- 4 tablespoons of barbecue spice rub
- 1 tablespoon kosher salt and black pepper
- 3 tablespoons brown sugar
- 2 pounds of beef ribs (3-3 1/2 pounds), cut in thirds
- 1 cup barbecue sauce

Directions:
1. In a small bowl, add salt, pepper, brown sugar, and BBQ spice rub.
2. Grease the ribs with oil spray from both sides and then rub it with a spice mixture.
3. Divide the ribs amongst the basket and set it to AIR FRY MODE at 375 degrees F for 15 minutes.
4. Hit start and let the air fryer cook the ribs.
5. Once done, serve with the coating BBQ sauce.

Nutrition Info:
- (Per serving) Calories 1081 | Fat 28.6 g| Sodium 1701mg | Carbs 58g | Fiber 0.8g| Sugar 45.7g | Protein 138 g

Curry-crusted Lamb Chops With Baked Brown Sugar Acorn Squash

Servings: 4
Cooking Time: 20 Minutes
Ingredients:
- FOR THE LAMB CHOPS
- 4 lamb loin chops (4 ounces each)
- 1 tablespoon olive oil
- 2 teaspoons curry powder
- ¼ teaspoon kosher salt
- FOR THE ACORN SQUASH
- 2 small acorn squash
- 4 teaspoons dark brown sugar
- 2 teaspoons salted butter
- ⅛ teaspoon kosher salt

Directions:
1. To prep the lamb chops: Brush both sides of the lamb chops with the oil and season with the curry powder and salt.
2. To prep the acorn squash: Cut the squash in half through the stem end and remove the seeds. Place 1 teaspoon of brown sugar and ½ teaspoon of butter into the well of each squash half.
3. To cook the lamb and squash: Install a crisper plate in each of the two baskets. Place the lamb chops in the Zone 1 basket and insert the basket in the unit. Place the squash cut-side up in the Zone 2 basket and insert the basket in the unit.
4. Select Zone 1, select AIR FRY, set the temperature to 400°F, and set the timer to 15 minutes.
5. Select Zone 2, select BAKE, set the temperature to 400°F, and set the time to 20 minutes. Select SMART FINISH.
6. Press START/PAUSE to begin cooking.
7. When both timers read 5 minutes, press START/PAUSE. Remove the Zone 1 basket and use a pair of silicone-tipped tongs to flip the lamb chops. Reinsert the basket in the unit. Remove the Zone 2 basket and spoon the melted butter and sugar over the top edges of the squash. Reinsert the basket and press START/PAUSE to resume cooking.
8. When cooking is complete, the lamb should be cooked to your liking and the squash soft when pierced with a fork.
9. Remove the lamb chops from the basket and let rest for 5 minutes. Season the acorn squash with salt before serving.

Nutrition Info:
- (Per serving) Calories: 328; Total fat: 19g; Saturated fat: 7.5g; Carbohydrates: 23g; Fiber: 3g; Protein: 16g; Sodium: 172mg

Korean Bbq Beef

Servings: 6
Cooking Time: 30 Minutes
Ingredients:
- For the meat:
- 1 pound flank steak or thinly sliced steak
- ¼ cup corn starch
- Coconut oil spray
- For the sauce:
- ½ cup soy sauce or gluten-free soy sauce
- ½ cup brown sugar
- 2 tablespoons white wine vinegar
- 1 clove garlic, crushed
- 1 tablespoon hot chili sauce
- 1 teaspoon ground ginger
- ½ teaspoon sesame seeds
- 1 tablespoon corn starch
- 1 tablespoon water

Directions:
1. To begin, prepare the steak. Thinly slice it in that toss it in the corn starch to be coated thoroughly. Spray the tops with some coconut oil.
2. Spray the crisping plates and drawers with the coconut oil.
3. Place the crisping plates into the drawers. Place the steak strips into each drawer. Insert both drawers into the unit.
4. Select zone 1, Select AIR FRY, set the temperature to 375 degrees F/ 190 degrees C, and set time to 30 minutes. Select MATCH to match zone 2 settings with zone 1. Press the START/STOP button to begin cooking.
5. While the steak is cooking, add the sauce ingredients EXCEPT for the corn starch and water to a medium saucepan.
6. Warm it up to a low boil, then whisk in the corn starch and water.
7. Carefully remove the steak and pour the sauce over. Mix well.

Nutrition Info:
- (Per serving) Calories 500 | Fat 19.8g | Sodium 680mg | Carbs 50.1g | Fiber 4.1g | Sugar 0g | Protein 27.9g

Ham Burger Patties

Servings: 2
Cooking Time: 17

Ingredients:
- 1 pound of ground beef
- Salt and pepper, to taste
- ½ teaspoon of red chili powder
- ¼ teaspoon of coriander powder
- 2 tablespoons of chopped onion
- 1 green chili, chopped
- Oil spray for greasing
- 2 large potato wedges

Directions:
1. Oil greases the air fryer baskets with oil spray.
2. Add potato wedges in the zone 1 basket.
3. Take a bowl and add minced beef in it and add salt, pepper, chili powder, coriander powder, green chili, and chopped onion.
4. mix well and make two burger patties with wet hands place the two patties in the air fryer zone 2 basket.
5. put the basket inside the air fryer.
6. now, set time for zone 1 for 12 minutes using AIR FRY mode at 400 degrees F.
7. Select the MATCH button for zone 2.
8. once the time of cooking complete, take out the baskets.
9. flip the patties and shake the potatoes wedges.
10. again, set time of zone 1 basket for 4 minutes at 400 degrees F
11. Select the MATCH button for the second basket.
12. Once it's done, serve and enjoy.

Nutrition Info:
- (Per serving) Calories875 | Fat21.5g | Sodium 622mg | Carbs 88g | Fiber10.9 g| Sugar 3.4g | Protein 78.8g

Yogurt Lamb Chops

Servings: 2
Cooking Time: 20

Ingredients:
- 1½ cups plain Greek yogurt
- 1 lemon, juice only
- 1 teaspoon ground cumin
- 1 teaspoon ground coriander
- ¾ teaspoon ground turmeric
- ¼ teaspoon ground allspice
- 10 rib lamb chops (1–1¼ inches thick cut)
- 2 tablespoons olive oil, divided

Directions:
1. Take a bowl and add lamb chop along with listed ingredients.
2. Rub the lamb chops well.
3. and let it marinate in the refrigerator for 1 hour.
4. Afterward takeout the lamb chops from the refrigerator.
5. Layer parchment paper on top of the baskets of the air fryer.
6. Divide it between ninja air fryer baskets.
7. Set the time for zone 1 to 20 minutes at 400 degrees F.
8. Select the MATCH button for the zone 2 basket.
9. Hit start and then wait for the chop to be cooked.
10. Once the cooking is done, the cool sign will appear on display.
11. Take out the lamb chops and let the chops serve on plates.

Nutrition Info:
- (Per serving) Calories1973 | Fat90 g| Sodium228 mg | Carbs 109.2g | Fiber 1g | Sugar 77.5g | Protein 184g

Balsamic Steak Tips With Roasted Asparagus And Mushroom Medley

Servings: 4
Cooking Time: 25 Minutes

Ingredients:
- FOR THE STEAK TIPS
- 1½ pounds sirloin tips
- ½ cup olive oil
- ¼ cup balsamic vinegar
- ¼ cup packed light brown sugar
- 1 tablespoon reduced-sodium soy sauce
- 1 teaspoon finely chopped fresh rosemary
- 1 teaspoon minced garlic
- FOR THE ASPARAGUS AND MUSHROOMS
- 6 ounces sliced cremini mushrooms
- 1 small red onion, sliced
- 1 tablespoon olive oil
- 1 pound asparagus, tough ends trimmed
- ⅛ teaspoon kosher salt

Directions:
1. To prep the steak tips: In a large bowl, combine the sirloin tips, oil, vinegar, brown sugar, soy sauce, rosemary, and garlic. Mix well to coat the steak.
2. To prep the mushrooms: In a large bowl, combine the mushrooms, onion, and oil.
3. To cook the steak and vegetables: Install a crisper plate in each of the two baskets. Shake any excess marinade from the steak tips, place the steak in the Zone 1 basket, and insert the basket in the unit. Place the mushrooms and onions in the Zone 2 basket and insert the basket in the unit.
4. Select Zone 1, select AIR FRY, set the temperature to 400°F, and set the time to 12 minutes.
5. Select Zone 2, select ROAST, set the temperature to 400°F, and set the time to 25 minutes. Select SMART FINISH.
6. Press START/PAUSE to begin cooking.
7. When the Zone 2 timer reads 10 minutes, press START/PAUSE. Remove the basket, add the asparagus to the mushrooms and onion, and sprinkle with salt. Reinsert the basket and press START/PAUSE to resume cooking.
8. When cooking is complete, the beef should be cooked to your liking and the asparagus crisp-tender. Serve warm.

Nutrition Info:
- (Per serving) Calories: 524; Total fat: 33g; Saturated fat: 2.5g; Carbohydrates: 16g; Fiber: 3g; Protein: 41g; Sodium: 192mg

Sausage Meatballs

Servings: 24
Cooking Time: 10 Minutes

Ingredients:
- 1 egg, lightly beaten
- 900g pork sausage
- 29g breadcrumbs
- 100g pimientos, drained & diced
- 1 tsp curry powder
- 1 tbsp garlic, minced
- 30ml olive oil
- 1 tbsp fresh rosemary, minced
- 25g parsley, minced
- Pepper
- Salt

Directions:
1. In a bowl, add pork sausage and remaining ingredients and mix until well combined.
2. Insert a crisper plate in the Ninja Foodi air fryer baskets.
3. Make small balls from the meat mixture and place them in both baskets.
4. Select zone 1 then select "air fry" mode and set the temperature to 390 degrees F for 10 minutes. Press "match" to match zone 2 settings to zone 1. Press "start/stop" to begin.

Nutrition Info:
- (Per serving) Calories 153 | Fat 12.2g | Sodium 303mg | Carbs 2.6g | Fiber 0.4g | Sugar 1.1g | Protein 8g

Pork Katsu With Seasoned Rice

Servings: 4
Cooking Time: 15 Minutes

Ingredients:
- FOR THE PORK KATSU
- 4 thin-sliced boneless pork chops (4 ounces each)
- 2 tablespoons all-purpose flour
- 2 large eggs
- 1 cup panko bread crumbs
- ¼ teaspoon kosher salt
- ¼ teaspoon freshly ground black pepper
- 1 teaspoon vegetable oil
- 3 tablespoons ketchup
- 3 tablespoons Worcestershire sauce
- 1 tablespoon oyster sauce
- ⅛ teaspoon granulated sugar
- FOR THE RICE
- 2 cups dried instant rice (not microwavable)
- 2½ cups water
- 1 tablespoon sesame oil
- 1 teaspoon soy sauce
- 1 tablespoon toasted sesame seeds
- 3 scallions, sliced

Directions:
1. To prep the pork katsu: Place the pork chops between two slices of plastic wrap. Using a meat mallet or rolling pin, pound the pork into ½-inch-thick cutlets.
2. Set up a breading station with three small shallow bowls. Place the flour in the first bowl. In the second bowl, whisk the eggs. Combine the panko, salt, and black pepper in the third bowl.
3. Bread the cutlets in this order: First, dip them in the flour, coating both sides. Then, dip them into the beaten egg. Finally, coat them in panko, gently pressing the bread crumbs to adhere to the pork. Drizzle both sides of the cutlets with the oil.
4. To prep the rice: In the Zone 2 basket, combine the rice, water, sesame oil, and soy sauce. Stir well to ensure all of the rice is submerged in the liquid.
5. To cook the pork and rice: Install a crisper plate in the Zone 1 basket. Place the pork in the basket and insert the basket in the unit. Insert the Zone 2 basket in the unit.
6. Select Zone 1, select AIR FRY, set the temperature to 390°F, and set the time to 15 minutes.
7. Select Zone 2, select BAKE, set the temperature to 350°F, and set the time to 10 minutes. Select SMART FINISH.
8. Press START/PAUSE to begin cooking.
9. When the Zone 1 timer reads 10 minutes, press START/PAUSE. Remove the basket and use silicone-tipped tongs to flip the pork. Reinsert the basket and press START/PAUSE to resume cooking.
10. When cooking is complete, the pork should be crisp and cooked through and the rice tender.
11. Stir the sesame seeds and scallions into the rice. For the sauce to go with the pork, in a small bowl, whisk together the ketchup, Worcestershire sauce, oyster sauce, and sugar. Drizzle the sauce over the pork and serve with the hot rice.

Nutrition Info:
- (Per serving) Calories: 563; Total fat: 20g; Saturated fat: 5.5g; Carbohydrates: 62g; Fiber: 1g; Protein: 34g; Sodium: 665mg

Beef Ribs Ii

Servings: 2
Cooking Time: 1
Ingredients:

- ¼ cup olive oil
- 4 garlic cloves, minced
- ½ cup white wine vinegar
- ¼ cup soy sauce, reduced-sodium
- ¼ cup Worcestershire sauce
- 1 lemon juice
- Salt and black pepper, to taste
- 2 tablespoons of Italian seasoning
- 1 teaspoon of smoked paprika
- 2 tablespoons of mustard
- ½ cup maple syrup
- Meat Ingredients:
- Oil spray, for greasing
- 8 beef ribs lean

Directions:
1. Take a large bowl and add all the ingredients under marinade ingredients.
2. Put the marinade in a zip lock bag and add ribs to it.
3. Let it sit for 4 hours.
4. Now take out the basket of air fryer and grease the baskets with oil spray.
5. Now dived the ribs among two baskets.
6. Set it to AIR fry mode at 220 degrees F for 30 minutes.
7. Select Pause and take out the baskets.
8. Afterward, flip the ribs and cook for 30 minutes at 250 degrees F.
9. Once done, serve the juicy and tender ribs.
10. Enjoy.

Nutrition Info:
- (Per serving) Calories 1927| Fat116g| Sodium 1394mg | Carbs 35.2g | Fiber 1.3g| Sugar29 g | Protein 172.3g

Lamb Chops With Dijon Garlic

Servings: 4
Cooking Time: 22 Minutes
Ingredients:

- 2 teaspoons Dijon mustard
- 2 teaspoons olive oil
- 1 teaspoon soy sauce
- 1 teaspoon garlic, minced
- 1 teaspoon cumin powder
- 1 teaspoon cayenne pepper
- 1 teaspoon Italian spice blend (optional)
- ¼ teaspoon salt
- 8 lamb chops

Directions:
1. Combine the Dijon mustard, olive oil, soy sauce, garlic, cumin powder, cayenne pepper, Italian spice blend (optional), and salt in a medium mixing bowl.
2. Put the marinade in a large Ziploc bag. Add the lamb chops. Seal the bag tightly after pressing out the air. Coat the lamb in the marinade by shaking the bag and pressing the chops into the mixture. Place in the fridge for at least 30 minutes, or up to overnight, to marinate.
3. Install a crisper plate in both drawers. Place half the lamb chops in the zone 1 drawer and half in zone 2's, then insert the drawers into the unit.
4. Select zone 1, select AIR FRY, set temperature to 390 degrees F/ 200 degrees C, and set time to 22 minutes. Select MATCH to match zone 2 settings to zone 1. Press the START/STOP button to begin cooking.
5. When the time reaches 11 minutes, press START/STOP to pause the unit. Remove the drawers and flip the lamb chops. Re-insert the drawers into the unit and press START/STOP to resume cooking.
6. Serve and enjoy!

Nutrition Info:
- (Per serving) Calories 343 | Fat 15.1g | Sodium 380mg | Carbs 0.9 g | Fiber 0.3g | Sugar 0.1g | Protein 48.9g

Steak And Asparagus Bundles

Servings: 6
Cooking Time: 10 Minutes

Ingredients:
- 907g flank steak, cut into 6 pieces
- Salt and black pepper, to taste
- ½ cup tamari sauce
- 2 cloves garlic, crushed
- 455g asparagus, trimmed
- 3 capsicums, sliced
- ¼ cup balsamic vinegar
- 79 ml beef broth
- 2 tablespoons unsalted butter
- Olive oil spray

Directions:
1. Mix steaks with black pepper, tamari sauce, and garlic in a Ziplock bag.
2. Seal the bag, shake well and refrigerate for 1 hour.
3. Place the steaks on the working surface and top each with asparagus and capsicums.
4. Roll the steaks and secure them with toothpicks.
5. Place these rolls in the air fryer baskets.
6. Return the air fryer basket 1 to Zone 1, and basket 2 to Zone 2 of the Ninja Foodi 2-Basket Air Fryer.
7. Choose the "Air Fry" mode for Zone 1 and set the temperature to 400 degrees F and 10 minutes of cooking time.
8. Select the "MATCH COOK" option to copy the settings for Zone 2.
9. Initiate cooking by pressing the START/PAUSE BUTTON.
10. Meanwhile, cook broth with butter and vinegar in a saucepan.
11. Cook this mixture until reduced by half and adjust seasoning with black pepper and salt.
12. Serve the steak rolls with the prepared sauce.

Nutrition Info:
- (Per serving) Calories 551 | Fat 31g | Sodium 1329mg | Carbs 1½g | Fiber 0.8g | Sugar 0.4g | Protein 64g

Paprika Pork Chops

Servings: 4
Cooking Time: 12 Minutes

Ingredients:
- 4 bone-in pork chops (6–8 ounces each)
- 1½ tablespoons brown sugar
- 1¼ teaspoons kosher salt
- 1 teaspoon dried Italian seasoning
- 1 teaspoon smoked paprika
- ¼ teaspoon garlic powder
- ¼ teaspoon onion powder
- ¼ teaspoon black pepper
- 1 teaspoon sweet paprika
- 3 tablespoons butter, melted
- 2 tablespoons chopped fresh parsley
- Cooking spray

Directions:
1. In a small mixing bowl, combine the brown sugar, salt, Italian seasoning, smoked paprika, garlic powder, onion powder, black pepper, and sweet paprika. Mix thoroughly.
2. Brush the pork chops on both sides with the melted butter.
3. Rub the spice mixture all over the meat on both sides.
4. Install a crisper plate in both drawers. Place half the chops in the zone 1 drawer and half in zone 2's, then insert the drawers into the unit.
5. Select zone 1, select AIR FRY, set temperature to 390 degrees F/ 200 degrees C, and set time to 12 minutes. Select MATCH to match zone 2 settings to zone 1. Press the START/STOP button to begin cooking.
6. When the time reaches 10 minutes, press START/STOP to pause the unit. Remove the drawers and flip the chops. Re-insert the drawers into the unit and press START/STOP to resume cooking.
7. Serve and enjoy!

Nutrition Info:
- (Per serving) Calories 338 | Fat 21.2g | Sodium 1503mg | Carbs 5.1g | Fiber 0.3g | Sugar 4.6g | Protein 29.3g

Pork With Green Beans And Potatoes

Servings: 4
Cooking Time: 15 Minutes.
Ingredients:
- ¼ cup Dijon mustard
- 2 tablespoons brown sugar
- 1 teaspoon dried parsley flake
- ½ teaspoon dried thyme
- ¼ teaspoons salt
- ¼ teaspoons black pepper
- 1 ¼ lbs. pork tenderloin
- ¾ lb. small potatoes halved
- 1 (12-oz) package green beans, trimmed
- 1 tablespoon olive oil
- Salt and black pepper ground to taste

Directions:
1. Preheat your Air Fryer Machine to 400 degrees F.
2. Add mustard, parsley, brown sugar, salt, black pepper, and thyme in a large bowl, then mix well.
3. Add tenderloin to the spice mixture and coat well.
4. Toss potatoes with olive oil, salt, black pepper, and green beans in another bowl.
5. Place the prepared tenderloin in the crisper plate.
6. Return this crisper plate to the Zone 1 of the Ninja Foodi Dual Zone Air Fryer.
7. Choose the Air Fry mode for Zone 1 and set the temperature to 390 degrees F and the time to 15 minutes.
8. Add potatoes and green beans to the Zone 2.
9. Choose the Air Fry mode for Zone 2 with 350 degrees F and the time to 10 minutes.
10. Press the SYNC button to sync the finish time for both Zones.
11. Initiate cooking by pressing the START/STOP button.
12. Serve the tenderloin with Air Fried potatoes

Nutrition Info:
- (Per serving) Calories 400 | Fat 32g | Sodium 721mg | Carbs 2.6g | Fiber 0g | Sugar 0g | Protein 27.4g

Bbq Pork Chops

Servings: 4
Cooking Time: 12 Minutes
Ingredients:
- 4 pork chops
- Salt and black pepper to taste
- 1 package BBQ Shake & Bake
- Olive oil

Directions:
1. Season pork chops with black pepper, salt, BBQ shake and olive oil.
2. Place these chops in the air fryer baskets.
3. Return the air fryer basket 1 to Zone 1, and basket 2 to Zone 2 of the Ninja Foodi 2-Basket Air Fryer.
4. Choose the "Air Fry" mode for Zone 1 at 375 degrees F and 12 minutes of cooking time.
5. Select the "MATCH COOK" option to copy the settings for Zone 2.
6. Initiate cooking by pressing the START/PAUSE BUTTON.
7. Flip the pork chops once cooked halfway through.
8. Serve warm.

Nutrition Info:
- (Per serving) Calories 437 | Fat 28g | Sodium 1221mg | Carbs 22.3g | Fiber 0.9g | Sugar 8g | Protein 30.3g

Mongolian Beef With Sweet Chili Brussels Sprouts

Servings: 4
Cooking Time: 20 Minutes

Ingredients:
- FOR THE MONGOLIAN BEEF
- 1 pound flank steak, cut into thin strips
- 1 tablespoon olive oil
- 2 tablespoons cornstarch
- ½ cup reduced-sodium soy sauce
- ½ cup packed light brown sugar
- 1 tablespoon chili paste (optional)
- 1 tablespoon minced garlic
- 1 tablespoon minced fresh ginger
- 2 scallions, chopped
- FOR THE BRUSSELS SPROUTS
- 1 pound Brussels sprouts, halved lengthwise
- 1 tablespoon olive oil
- ½ cup gochujang sauce
- 2 tablespoons rice vinegar
- 1 tablespoon reduced-sodium soy sauce
- 1 tablespoon light brown sugar
- 1 teaspoon fresh garlic

Directions:
1. To prep the Mongolian beef: In a large bowl, combine the flank steak and olive oil and toss to coat. Add the cornstarch and toss to coat.
2. In a small bowl, whisk together the soy sauce, brown sugar, chili paste (if using), garlic, and ginger. Set the soy sauce mixture aside.
3. To prep the Brussels sprouts: In a large bowl, combine the Brussels sprouts and oil and toss to coat.
4. In a small bowl, whisk together the gochujang sauce, vinegar, soy sauce, brown sugar, and garlic. Set the chili sauce mixture aside.
5. To cook the beef and Brussels sprouts: Install a crisper plate in each of the two baskets. Place the beef in the Zone 1 basket and insert the basket in the unit. Place the Brussels sprouts in the Zone 2 basket and insert the basket in the unit.
6. Select Zone 1, select AIR FRY, set the temperature to 390°F, and set the time to 15 minutes.
7. Select Zone 2, select AIR FRY, set the temperature to 400°F, and set the time to 20 minutes. Select SMART FINISH.
8. Press START/PAUSE to begin cooking.
9. When both timers read 5 minutes, press START/PAUSE. Remove the Zone 1 basket, add the reserved soy sauce mixture and the scallions, and toss with the beef. Reinsert the basket. Remove the Zone 2 basket, add the reserved chili sauce mixture, and toss with the Brussels sprouts. Reinsert the basket and press START/PAUSE to resume cooking.
10. When cooking is complete, the steak should be cooked through and the Brussels sprouts tender and slightly caramelized. Serve warm.

Nutrition Info:
- (Per serving) Calories: 481; Total fat: 16g; Saturated fat: 4.5g; Carbohydrates: 60g; Fiber: 5g; Protein: 27g; Sodium: 2,044mg

Pork Chops With Brussels Sprouts

Servings: 4
Cooking Time: 15 Minutes.
Ingredients:
- 4 bone-in center-cut pork chop
- Cooking spray
- Salt, to taste
- Black pepper, to taste
- 2 teaspoons olive oil
- 2 teaspoons pure maple syrup
- 2 teaspoons Dijon mustard
- 6 ounces Brussels sprouts, quartered

Directions:
1. Rub pork chop with salt, ¼ teaspoons black pepper, and cooking spray.
2. Toss Brussels sprouts with mustard, syrup, oil, ¼ teaspoon of black pepper in a medium bowl.
3. Add pork chop to the crisper plate of Zone 1 of the Ninja Foodi Dual Zone Air Fryer.
4. Return the crisper plate to the Ninja Foodi Dual Zone Air Fryer.
5. Choose the Air Fry mode for Zone 1 and set the temperature to 400 degrees F and the time to 15 minutes.
6. Add the Brussels sprouts to the crisper plate of Zone 2 and return it to the unit.
7. Choose the Air Fry mode for Zone 2 with 350 degrees F and the time to 13 minutes.
8. Press the SYNC button to sync the finish time for both Zones.
9. Initiate cooking by pressing the START/STOP button.
10. Serve warm and fresh

Nutrition Info:
- (Per serving) Calories 336 | Fat 27.1g |Sodium 66mg | Carbs 1.1g | Fiber 0.4g | Sugar 0.2g | Protein 19.7g

Tasty Pork Skewers

Servings: 3
Cooking Time: 10 Minutes
Ingredients:
- 450g pork shoulder, cut into ¼-inch pieces
- 66ml soy sauce
- ½ tbsp garlic, crushed
- 1 tbsp ginger paste
- 1 ½ tsp sesame oil
- 22ml rice vinegar
- 21ml honey
- Pepper
- Salt

Directions:
1. In a bowl, mix meat with the remaining ingredients. Cover and place in the refrigerator for 30 minutes.
2. Thread the marinated meat onto the soaked skewers.
3. Insert a crisper plate in the Ninja Foodi air fryer baskets.
4. Place the pork skewers in both baskets.
5. Select zone 1, then select "air fry" mode and set the temperature to 360 degrees F for 10 minutes. Press "match" and then press "start/stop" to begin. Turn halfway through.

Nutrition Info:
- (Per serving) Calories 520 | Fat 34.7g |Sodium 1507mg | Carbs 12.2g | Fiber 0.5g | Sugar 9.1g | Protein 37g

Poultry Recipes

Marinated Chicken Legs

Servings: 6
Cooking Time: 28 Minutes
Ingredients:
- 6 chicken legs
- 15ml olive oil
- 1 tsp ground mustard
- 36g brown sugar
- ¼ tsp cayenne
- 1 tsp smoked paprika
- 1 tsp garlic powder
- 1 tsp onion powder
- Pepper
- Salt

Directions:
1. Add the chicken legs and the remaining ingredients into a zip-lock bag. Seal the bag and place in the refrigerator for 4 hours.
2. Insert a crisper plate in the Ninja Foodi air fryer baskets.
3. Place the marinated chicken legs in both baskets.
4. Select zone 1, then select "bake" mode and set the temperature to 390 degrees F for 25-28 minutes. Press "match" to match zone 2 settings to zone 1. Press "start/stop" to begin.

Nutrition Info:
- (Per serving) Calories 308 | Fat 17.9g |Sodium 128mg | Carbs 5.5g | Fiber 0.3g | Sugar 4.7g | Protein 29.9g

Glazed Thighs With French Fries

Servings:3
Cooking Time:35
Ingredients:
- 2 tablespoons of Soy Sauce
- Salt, to taste
- 1 teaspoon of Worcestershire Sauce
- 2 teaspoons Brown Sugar
- 1 teaspoon of Ginger, paste
- 1 teaspoon of Garlic, paste
- 6 Boneless Chicken Thighs
- 1 pound of hand-cut potato fries
- 2 tablespoons of canola oil

Directions:
1. Coat the French fries well with canola oil.
2. Season it with salt.
3. In a small bowl, combine the soy sauce, Worcestershire sauce, brown sugar, ginger, and garlic.
4. Place the chicken in this marinade and let it sit for 40 minutes.
5. Put the chicken thighs into the zone 1 basket and fries into the zone 2 basket.
6. Press button 1 for the first basket, and set it to ROAST mode at 350 degrees F for 35 minutes.
7. For the second basket hit 2 and set time to 30 minutes at 360 degrees F, by selecting AIR FRY mode.
8. Once the cooking cycle completely take out the fries and chicken and serve it hot.

Nutrition Info:
- (Per serving) Calories 858| Fat39g | Sodium 1509mg | Carbs 45.6g | Fiber 4.4g | Sugar3 g | Protein 90g

Thai Chicken Meatballs

Servings: 4
Cooking Time: 10 Minutes
Ingredients:
- ½ cup sweet chili sauce
- 2 tablespoons lime juice
- 2 tablespoons ketchup
- 1 teaspoon soy sauce
- 1 large egg, lightly beaten
- ¾ cup panko breadcrumbs
- 1 green onion, finely chopped
- 1 tablespoon minced fresh cilantro
- ½ teaspoon salt
- ½ teaspoon garlic powder
- 1-pound lean ground chicken

Directions:
1. Combine the chili sauce, lime juice, ketchup, and soy sauce in a small bowl; set aside ½ cup for serving.
2. Combine the egg, breadcrumbs, green onion, cilantro, salt, garlic powder, and the remaining 4 tablespoons chili sauce mixture in a large mixing bowl. Mix in the chicken lightly yet thoroughly. Form into 12 balls.
3. Install a crisper plate in both drawers. Place half the chicken meatballs in the zone 1 drawer and half in zone 2's, then insert the drawers into the unit.
4. Select zone 1, select AIR FRY, set temperature to 390 degrees F/ 200 degrees C, and set time to 10 minutes. Select MATCH to match zone 2 settings to zone 1. Press the START/STOP button to begin cooking.
5. When the time reaches 5 minutes, press START/STOP to pause the unit. Remove the drawers and flip the chicken. Re-insert the drawers into the unit and press START/STOP to resume cooking.
6. When cooking is complete, remove the chicken meatballs and serve hot.

Nutrition Info:
- (Per serving) Calories 93 | Fat 3g | Sodium 369mg | Carbs 9g | Fiber 0g | Sugar 6g | Protein 9g

Italian Chicken & Potatoes

Servings: 4
Cooking Time: 24 Minutes
Ingredients:
- 450g chicken breast, boneless & diced
- 30ml olive oil
- ½ tsp lemon zest
- 2 tbsp fresh lemon juice
- 450g baby potatoes, quartered
- 1 tbsp Greek seasoning
- Pepper
- Salt

Directions:
1. Toss potatoes with ½ tablespoon Greek seasoning, 1 tablespoon oil, lemon zest, lemon juice, pepper, and salt in a bowl.
2. Insert a crisper plate in the Ninja Foodi air fryer baskets.
3. Add potatoes into the zone 1 basket.
4. In a bowl, toss chicken with the remaining oil and seasoning.
5. Add the chicken into the zone 2 basket.
6. Select zone 1, then select "air fry" mode and set the temperature to 390 degrees F for 12 minutes. Press "match" to match zone 2 settings to zone 1. Press "start/stop" to begin.

Nutrition Info:
- (Per serving) Calories 262 | Fat 10.1g | Sodium 227mg | Carbs 15.5g | Fiber 2.9g | Sugar 0.2g | Protein 27.2g

Bbq Cheddar-stuffed Chicken Breasts

Servings: 2
Cooking Time: 25 Minutes
Ingredients:
- 3 strips cooked bacon, divided
- 2 ounces cheddar cheese, cubed, divided
- ¼ cup BBQ sauce, divided
- 2 (4-ounces) skinless, boneless chicken breasts
- Salt and ground black pepper, to taste

Directions:
1. In a mixing bowl, combine the cooked bacon, cheddar cheese, and 1 tablespoon BBQ sauce.
2. Make a horizontal 1-inch cut at the top of each chicken breast with a long, sharp knife, producing a little interior pouch. Fill each breast with an equal amount of the bacon-cheese mixture. Wrap the remaining bacon strips around each chicken breast. Coat the chicken breasts with the leftover BBQ sauce and lay them in a baking dish.
3. Install a crisper plate in both drawers. Place half the chicken breasts in zone 1 and half in zone 2, then insert the drawers into the unit.
4. Select zone 1, select AIR FRY, set temperature to 390 degrees F/ 200 degrees C, and set time to 22 minutes. Select MATCH to match zone 2 settings to zone 1. Press the START/STOP button to begin cooking.
5. When the time reaches 11 minutes, press START/STOP to pause the unit. Remove the drawers and flip the chicken. Re-insert drawers into the unit and press START/STOP to resume cooking.
6. When cooking is complete, remove the chicken breasts.

Nutrition Info:
- (Per serving) Calories 379 | Fat 12.8g | Sodium 906mg | Carbs 11.1g | Fiber 0.4g | Sugar 8.3g | Protein 37.7g

Chicken And Potatoes

Servings: 2
Cooking Time: 10 Minutes
Ingredients:
- 2 potatoes, diced
- 2 chicken breasts, diced
- 4 cloves garlic crushed
- 2 teaspoons smoked paprika
- ½ teaspoon red chili flakes
- 1 teaspoon fresh thyme
- 1 teaspoon salt
- ¼ teaspoon black pepper
- 2 tablespoons olive oil

Directions:
1. Rub chicken with half of the salt, black pepper, oil, thyme, red chili flakes, paprika and garlic.
2. Mix potatoes with remaining spices, oil and garlic in a bowl.
3. Add chicken to one air fryer basket and potatoes the second basket.
4. Return the air fryer basket 1 to Zone 1, and basket 2 to Zone 2 of the Ninja Foodi 2-Basket Air Fryer.
5. Choose the "Air Fry" mode for Zone 1 at 375 degrees F and 10 minutes of cooking time.
6. Select the "MATCH COOK" option to copy the settings for Zone 2.
7. Initiate cooking by pressing the START/PAUSE BUTTON.
8. Flip the chicken and toss potatoes once cooked halfway through.
9. Garnish with chopped parsley.
10. Serve chicken with the potatoes.

Nutrition Info:
- (Per serving) Calories 374 | Fat 13g |Sodium 552mg | Carbs 25g | Fiber 1.2g | Sugar 1.2g | Protein 37.7g

Cornish Hen

Servings: 4
Cooking Time: 35 Minutes

Ingredients:

- 2 Cornish hens
- 2 tablespoons olive oil
- 2 teaspoons salt
- 1½ teaspoons Italian seasoning
- 1 teaspoon garlic powder
- 1 teaspoon paprika
- ½ teaspoon black pepper
- ½ teaspoon lemon zest

Directions:

1. Mix Italian seasoning with lemon zest, juice, black pepper, paprika, and garlic powder in a bowl.
2. Rub each hen with the seasoning mixture.
3. Tuck the hen wings in and place one in each air fryer basket.
4. Return the air fryer basket 1 to Zone 1, and basket 2 to Zone 2 of the Ninja Foodi 2-Basket Air Fryer.
5. Choose the "Air Fry" mode for Zone 1 and set the temperature to 375 degrees F and 35 minutes of cooking time.
6. Select the "MATCH COOK" option to copy the settings for Zone 2.
7. Initiate cooking by pressing the START/PAUSE BUTTON.
8. Flip the hens once cooked halfway through.
9. Serve warm.

Nutrition Info:

- (Per serving) Calories 223 | Fat 11.7g |Sodium 721mg | Carbs 13.6g | Fiber 0.7g | Sugar 8g | Protein 15.7g

Ranch Turkey Tenders With Roasted Vegetable Salad

Servings:4
Cooking Time: 20 Minutes

Ingredients:

- FOR THE TURKEY TENDERS
- 1 pound turkey tenderloin
- ¼ cup ranch dressing
- ½ cup panko bread crumbs
- Nonstick cooking spray
- FOR THE VEGETABLE SALAD
- 1 large sweet potato, peeled and diced
- 1 zucchini, diced
- 1 red bell pepper, diced
- 1 small red onion, sliced
- 1 tablespoon vegetable oil
- ¼ teaspoon kosher salt
- ½ teaspoon freshly ground black pepper
- 2 cups baby spinach
- ½ cup store-bought balsamic vinaigrette
- ¼ cup chopped walnuts

Directions:

1. To prep the turkey tenders: Slice the turkey crosswise into 16 strips. Brush both sides of each strip with ranch dressing, then coat with the panko. Press the bread crumbs into the turkey to help them adhere. Mist both sides of the strips with cooking spray.
2. To prep the vegetables: In a large bowl, combine the sweet potato, zucchini, bell pepper, onion, and vegetable oil. Stir well to coat the vegetables. Season with the salt and black pepper.
3. To cook the turkey and vegetables: Install a crisper plate in the Zone 1 basket. Place the turkey tenders in the basket in a single layer and insert the basket in the unit. Place the vegetables in the Zone 2 basket and insert the basket in the unit.
4. Select Zone 1, select AIR FRY, set the temperature to 375°F, and set the time to 20 minutes.
5. Select Zone 2, select ROAST, set the temperature to 400°F, and set the time to 20 minutes. Select SMART FINISH.
6. Press START/PAUSE to begin cooking.
7. When both timers read 10 minutes, press START/PAUSE. Remove the Zone 1 basket and use silicone-tipped tongs to flip the turkey tenders. Reinsert the basket in the unit. Remove the Zone 2 basket and shake to redistribute the vegetables. Reinsert the basket and press START/PAUSE to resume cooking.
8. When cooking is complete, the turkey will be golden brown and cooked through (an instant-read thermometer should read 165°F) and the vegetables will be fork-tender.
9. Place the spinach in a large serving bowl. Mix in the roasted vegetables and balsamic vinaigrette. Sprinkle with walnuts. Serve warm with the turkey tenders.

Nutrition Info:

- (Per serving) Calories: 470; Total fat: 28g; Saturated fat: 2.5g; Carbohydrates: 28g; Fiber: 4g; Protein: 31g; Sodium: 718mg

Balsamic Duck Breast

Servings: 2
Cooking Time: 20 Minutes.

Ingredients:
- 2 duck breasts
- 1 teaspoon parsley
- Salt and black pepper, to taste
- Marinade:
- 1 tablespoon olive oil
- ½ teaspoon French mustard
- 1 teaspoon dried garlic
- 2 teaspoons honey
- ½ teaspoon balsamic vinegar

Directions:
1. Mix olive oil, mustard, garlic, honey, and balsamic vinegar in a bowl.
2. Add duck breasts to the marinade and rub well.
3. Place one duck breast in each crisper plate.
4. Return the crisper plates to the Ninja Foodi Dual Zone Air Fryer.
5. Choose the Air Fry mode for Zone 1 and set the temperature to 360 degrees F and the time to 20 minutes.
6. Select the "MATCH" button to copy the settings for Zone 2.
7. Initiate cooking by pressing the START/STOP button.
8. Flip the duck breasts once cooked halfway through, then resume cooking.
9. Serve warm.

Nutrition Info:
- (Per serving) Calories 546 | Fat 33.1g | Sodium 1201mg | Carbs 30g | Fiber 2.4g | Sugar 9.7g | Protein 32g

Chicken Parmesan

Servings: 4
Cooking Time: 20 Minutes

Ingredients:
- 2 large eggs
- ½ cup seasoned breadcrumbs
- 1/3 cup grated parmesan cheese
- ¼ teaspoon pepper
- 4 boneless, skinless chicken breast halves (6 ounces each)
- 1 cup pasta sauce
- 1 cup shredded mozzarella cheese
- Chopped fresh basil (optional)

Directions:
1. Lightly beat the eggs in a small bowl.
2. Combine the breadcrumbs, parmesan cheese, and pepper in a shallow bowl.
3. After dipping the chicken in the egg, coat it in the crumb mixture.
4. Install a crisper plate in both drawers. Place half the chicken breasts in the zone 1 drawer and half in zone 2's, then insert the drawers into the unit.
5. Select zone 1, select AIR FRY, set temperature to 390 degrees F/ 200 degrees C, and set time to 20 minutes. Select MATCH to match zone 2 settings to zone 1. Press the START/STOP button to begin cooking.
6. When the time reaches 10 minutes, press START/STOP to pause the unit. Remove the drawers and flip the chicken. Re-insert the drawers into the unit and press START/STOP to resume cooking.
7. When cooking is complete, remove the chicken.

Nutrition Info:
- (Per serving) Calories 293 | Fat 15.8g | Sodium 203mg | Carbs 11.1g | Fiber 2.4g | Sugar 8.7g | Protein 29g

Veggie Stuffed Chicken Breasts

Servings: 2
Cooking Time: 10 Minutes.

Ingredients:
- 4 teaspoons chili powder
- 4 teaspoons ground cumin
- 1 skinless, boneless chicken breast
- 2 teaspoons chipotle flakes
- 2 teaspoons Mexican oregano
- Salt and black pepper, to taste
- ½ red bell pepper, julienned
- ½ onion, julienned
- 1 fresh jalapeno pepper, julienned
- 2 teaspoons corn oil
- ½ lime, juiced

Directions:
1. Slice the chicken breast in half horizontally.
2. Pound each chicken breast with a mallet into ¼ inch thickness.
3. Rub the pounded chicken breast with black pepper, salt, oregano, chipotle flakes, cumin, and chili powder.
4. Add ½ of bell pepper, jalapeno, and onion on top of each chicken breast piece.
5. Roll the chicken to wrap the filling inside and insert toothpicks to seal.
6. Place the rolls in crisper plate and spray them with cooking oil.
7. Return the crisper plate to the Ninja Foodi Dual Zone Air Fryer.
8. Choose the Air Fry mode for Zone 1 and set the temperature to 360 degrees F and the time to 10 minutes.
9. Initiate cooking by pressing the START/STOP button.
10. Serve warm.

Nutrition Info:
- (Per serving) Calories 351 | Fat 11g |Sodium 150mg | Carbs 3.3g | Fiber 0.2g | Sugar 1g | Protein 33.2g

Wings With Corn On Cob

Servings:2
Cooking Time:40

Ingredients:
- 6 chicken wings, skinless
- 2 tablespoons of coconut amino
- 2 tablespoons of brown sugar
- 1 teaspoon of ginger, paste
- ½ inch garlic, minced
- Salt and black pepper to taste
- 2 corn on cobs, small
- Oil spray, for greasing

Directions:
1. Spay the corns with oil spray and season them with salt.
2. Rub the ingredients well.
3. Coat the chicken wings with coconut amino, brown sugar, ginger, garlic, salt, and black pepper.
4. Spray the wings with a good amount of oil spray.
5. Now put the chicken wings in the zone 1 basket.
6. Put the corn into the zone 2 basket.
7. Select ROAST function for chicken wings, press 1, and set time to 23 minutes at 400 degrees F.
8. Press 2 and select the AIR FRY function for corn and set the timer to 40 at 300 degrees F.
9. Once it's done, serve and enjoy.

Nutrition Info:
- (Per serving) Calories 950| Fat33.4g | Sodium592 mg | Carbs27. 4g | Fiber2.1g | Sugar11.3 g | Protein129 g

General Tso's Chicken

Servings: 4
Cooking Time: 22 Minutes.

Ingredients:

- 1 egg, large
- ⅓ cup 2 teaspoons cornstarch,
- ¼ teaspoons salt
- ¼ teaspoons ground white pepper
- 7 tablespoons chicken broth
- 2 tablespoons soy sauce
- 2 tablespoons ketchup
- 2 teaspoons sugar
- 2 teaspoons unseasoned rice vinegar
- 1 ½ tablespoons canola oil
- 4 chile de árbol, chopped and seeds discarded
- 1 tablespoon chopped fresh ginger
- 1 tablespoon garlic, chopped
- 2 tablespoons green onion, sliced
- 1 teaspoon toasted sesame oil
- 1 lb. boneless chicken thighs, cut into 1 ¼ -inch chunks
- ½ teaspoon toasted sesame seeds

Directions:

1. Add egg to a large bowl and beat it with a fork.
2. Add chicken to the egg and coat it well.
3. Whisk ⅓ cup of cornstarch with black pepper and salt in a small bowl.
4. Add chicken to the cornstarch mixture and mix well to coat.
5. Divide the chicken in the two crisper plates and spray them cooking oi.
6. Return the crisper plates to the Ninja Foodi Dual Zone Air Fryer.
7. Choose the Air Fry mode for Zone 1 and set the temperature to 390 degrees F and the time to 20 minutes.
8. Select the "MATCH" button to copy the settings for Zone 2.
9. Initiate cooking by pressing the START/STOP button.
10. Once done, remove the air fried chicken from the air fryer.
11. Whisk 2 teaspoons of cornstarch with soy sauce, broth, sugar, ketchup, and rice vinegar in a small bowl.
12. Add chilies and canola oil to a skillet and sauté for 1 minute.
13. Add garlic and ginger, then sauté for 30 seconds.
14. Stir in cornstarch sauce and cook until it bubbles and thickens.
15. Toss in cooked chicken and garnish with sesame oil, sesame seeds, and green onion.
16. Enjoy.

Nutrition Info:

- (Per serving) Calories 351 | Fat 16g |Sodium 777mg | Carbs 26g | Fiber 4g | Sugar 5g | Protein 28g

Juicy Duck Breast

Servings: 1
Cooking Time: 20 Minutes

Ingredients:

- ½ duck breast
- Salt and black pepper, to taste
- 2 tablespoons plum sauce

Directions:

1. Rub the duck breast with black pepper and salt.
2. Place the duck breast in air fryer basket 1 and add plum sauce on top.
3. Return the basket to the Ninja Foodi 2 Baskets Air Fryer.
4. Choose the "Air Fry" mode for Zone 1 and set the temperature to 400 degrees F and 20 minutes of cooking time.
5. Initiate cooking by pressing the START/PAUSE BUTTON.
6. Flip the duck breast once cooked halfway through.
7. Serve warm.

Nutrition Info:

- (Per serving) Calories 379 | Fat 19g |Sodium 184mg | Carbs 12.3g | Fiber 0.6g | Sugar 2g | Protein 37.7g

Chicken Leg Piece

Servings:1
Cooking Time:25
Ingredients:

- 1 teaspoon of onion powder
- 1 teaspoon of paprika powder
- 1 teaspoon of garlic powder
- Salt and black pepper, to taste
- 1 tablespoon of Italian seasoning
- 1 teaspoon of celery seeds
- 2 eggs, whisked
- 1/3 cup buttermilk
- 1 cup of corn flour
- 1 pound of chicken leg

Directions:
1. Take a bowl and whisk egg along with pepper, salt, and buttermilk.
2. Set it aside for further use.
3. Mix all the spices in a small separate bowl.
4. Dredge the chicken in egg wash then dredge it in seasoning.
5. Coat the chicken legs with oil spray.
6. At the end dust it with the corn flour.
7. Divide the leg pieces into two zones.
8. Set zone 1 basket to 400 degrees F, for 25 minutes.
9. Select MATCH for zone 2 basket.
10. Let the air fryer do the magic.
11. Once it's done, serve and enjoy.

Nutrition Info:
- (Per serving) Calories 1511| Fat 52.3g| Sodium615 mg | Carbs 100g | Fiber 9.2g | Sugar 8.1g | Protein 154.2g

Yummy Chicken Breasts

Servings:2
Cooking Time:25
Ingredients:

- 4 large chicken breasts, 6 ounces each
- 2 tablespoons of oil bay seasoning
- 1 tablespoon Montreal chicken seasoning
- 1 teaspoon of thyme
- 1/2 teaspoon of paprika
- Salt, to taste
- oil spray, for greasing

Directions:
1. Season the chicken breast pieces with the listed seasoning and let them rest for 40 minutes.
2. Grease both sides of the chicken breast pieces with oil spray.
3. Divide the chicken breast piece between both baskets.
4. Set zone 1 to AIRFRY mode at 400 degrees F, for 15 minutes.
5. Select the MATCH button for another basket.
6. Select pause and take out the baskets and flip the chicken breast pieces, after 15 minutes.
7. Select the zones to 400 degrees F for 10 more minutes using the MATCH cook button.
8. Once it's done serve.

Nutrition Info:
- (Per serving) Calories 711| Fat 27.7g| Sodium 895mg | Carbs 1.6g | Fiber 0.4g | Sugar 0.1g | Protein 106.3g

Spicy Chicken Wings

Servings: 8
Cooking Time: 30 Minutes
Ingredients:
- 900g chicken wings
- 1 tsp black pepper
- 12g brown sugar
- 1 tbsp chilli powder
- 57g butter, melted
- 1 tsp smoked paprika
- 1 tsp garlic powder
- 1 tsp salt

Directions:
1. In a bowl, toss chicken wings with remaining ingredients until well coated.
2. Insert a crisper plate in the Ninja Foodi air fryer baskets.
3. Add the chicken wings to both baskets.
4. Select zone 1, then select "air fry" mode and set the temperature to 355 degrees F for 30 minutes. Press "match" to match zone 2 settings to zone 1. Press "start/stop" to begin. Turn halfway through.

Nutrition Info:
- (Per serving) Calories 276 | Fat 14.4g |Sodium 439mg | Carbs 2.2g | Fiber 0.5g | Sugar 1.3g | Protein 33.1g

Chicken & Veggies

Servings: 4
Cooking Time: 10 Minutes
Ingredients:
- 450g chicken breast, boneless & cut into pieces
- 2 garlic cloves, minced
- 15ml olive oil
- 239g frozen mix vegetables
- 1 tbsp Italian seasoning
- ½ tsp chilli powder
- ½ tsp garlic powder
- Pepper
- Salt

Directions:
1. In a bowl, toss chicken with remaining ingredients until well coated.
2. Insert a crisper plate in the Ninja Foodi air fryer baskets.
3. Add chicken and vegetables in both baskets.
4. Select zone 1 then select "air fry" mode and set the temperature to 390 degrees F for 10 minutes. Press "match" to match zone 2 settings to zone 1. Press "start/stop" to begin.

Nutrition Info:
- (Per serving) Calories 221 | Fat 7.6g |Sodium 126mg | Carbs 10.6g | Fiber 3.3g | Sugar 2.7g | Protein 26.3g

Goat Cheese–stuffed Chicken Breast With Broiled Zucchini And Cherry Tomatoes

Servings: 4
Cooking Time: 25 Minutes

Ingredients:

- FOR THE STUFFED CHICKEN BREASTS
- 2 ounces soft goat cheese
- 1 tablespoon minced fresh parsley
- ½ teaspoon minced garlic
- 4 boneless, skinless chicken breasts (6 ounces each)
- 1 tablespoon vegetable oil
- ½ teaspoon Italian seasoning
- ½ teaspoon kosher salt
- ½ teaspoon freshly ground black pepper
- FOR THE ZUCCHINI AND TOMATOES
- 1 pound zucchini, diced
- 1 cup cherry tomatoes, halved
- 1 tablespoon vegetable oil
- ½ teaspoon kosher salt
- ¼ teaspoon freshly ground black pepper

Directions:

1. To prep the stuffed chicken breasts: In a small bowl, combine the goat cheese, parsley, and garlic. Mix well.
2. Cut a deep slit into the fatter side of each chicken breast to create a pocket (taking care to not go all the way through). Stuff each breast with the goat cheese mixture. Use a toothpick to secure the opening of the chicken, if needed.
3. Brush the outside of the chicken breasts with the oil and season with the Italian seasoning, salt, and black pepper.
4. To prep the zucchini and tomatoes: In a large bowl, combine the zucchini, tomatoes, and oil. Mix to coat. Season with salt and black pepper.
5. To cook the chicken and vegetables: Install a crisper plate in each of the two baskets. Insert a broil rack in the Zone 2 basket over the crisper plate. Place the chicken in the Zone 1 basket and insert the basket in the unit. Place the vegetables on the broiler rack in the Zone 2 basket and insert the basket in the unit.
6. Select Zone 1, select AIR FRY, set the temperature to 390°F, and set the time to 25 minutes.
7. Select Zone 2, select AIR BROIL, set the temperature to 450°F, and set the time to 10 minutes. Select SMART FINISH.
8. Press START/PAUSE to begin cooking.
9. When cooking is complete, the chicken will be golden brown and cooked through (an instant-read thermometer should read 165°F) and the zucchini will be soft and slightly charred. Serve hot.

Nutrition Info:

- (Per serving) Calories: 330; Total fat: 15g; Saturated fat: 4g; Carbohydrates: 5g; Fiber: 1.5g; Protein: 42g; Sodium: 409mg

Honey-cajun Chicken Thighs

Servings: 6
Cooking Time: 25 Minutes

Ingredients:

- ½ cup buttermilk
- 1 teaspoon hot sauce
- 1½ pounds skinless, boneless chicken thighs
- ¼ cup all-purpose flour
- ⅓ cup tapioca flour
- 2 ½ teaspoons Cajun seasoning
- ½ teaspoon garlic salt
- ½ teaspoon honey powder
- ¼ teaspoon ground paprika
- ⅛ teaspoon cayenne pepper
- 4 teaspoons honey

Directions:

1. In a resealable plastic bag, combine the buttermilk and hot sauce. Marinate the chicken thighs in the bag for 30 minutes.
2. Combine the flour, tapioca flour, Cajun spice, garlic salt, honey powder, paprika, and cayenne pepper in a small mixing bowl.
3. Remove the thighs from the buttermilk mixture and dredge them in the flour. Remove any excess flour by shaking it off.
4. Install a crisper plate in both drawers. Place half the chicken thighs in the zone 1 drawer and half in zone 2's, then insert the drawers into the unit.
5. Select zone 1, select AIR FRY, set temperature to 390 degrees F/ 200 degrees C, and set time to 25 minutes. Select MATCH to match zone 2 settings to zone 1. Press the START/STOP button to begin cooking.
6. When the time reaches 11 minutes, press START/STOP to pause the unit. Remove the drawers and flip the chicken. Re-insert the drawers into the unit and press START/STOP to resume cooking.
7. When cooking is complete, remove the chicken and serve.

Nutrition Info:

- (Per serving) Calories 243 | Fat 11.8g | Sodium 203mg | Carbs 16.1g | Fiber 0.4g | Sugar 5.1g | Protein 19g

Roasted Garlic Chicken Pizza With Cauliflower "wings"

Servings: 4
Cooking Time: 25 Minutes
Ingredients:

- FOR THE PIZZA
- 2 prebaked rectangular pizza crusts or flatbreads
- 2 tablespoons olive oil
- 1 tablespoon minced garlic
- 1½ cups shredded part-skim mozzarella cheese
- 6 ounces boneless, skinless chicken breast, thinly sliced
- ¼ teaspoon red pepper flakes (optional)
- FOR THE CAULIFLOWER "WINGS"
- 4 cups cauliflower florets
- 1 tablespoon vegetable oil
- ½ cup Buffalo wing sauce

Directions:

1. To prep the pizza: Trim the pizza crusts to fit in the air fryer basket, if necessary.
2. Brush the top of each crust with the oil and sprinkle with the garlic. Top the crusts with the mozzarella, chicken, and red pepper flakes (if using).
3. To prep the cauliflower "wings": In a large bowl, combine the cauliflower and oil and toss to coat the florets.
4. To cook the pizza and "wings": Install a crisper plate in each of the two baskets. Place one pizza in the Zone 1 basket and insert the basket in the unit. Place the cauliflower in the Zone 2 basket and insert the basket in the unit.
5. Select Zone 1, select ROAST, set the temperature to 375°F, and set the time to 25 minutes.
6. Select Zone 2, select AIR FRY, set the temperature to 390°F, and set the time to 25 minutes. Select SMART FINISH.
7. Press START/PAUSE to begin cooking.
8. When the Zone 1 timer reads 13 minutes, press START/PAUSE. Remove the basket. Transfer the pizza to a cutting board (the chicken should be cooked through and the cheese melted and bubbling). Add the second pizza to the basket. Reinsert the basket in the unit and press START/PAUSE to resume cooking.
9. When the Zone 2 timer reads 5 minutes, press START/PAUSE. Remove the basket and add the Buffalo wing sauce to the cauliflower. Shake well to evenly coat the cauliflower in the sauce. Reinsert the basket and press START/PAUSE to resume cooking.
10. When cooking is complete, the cauliflower will be crisp on the outside and tender inside, and the chicken on the second pizza will be cooked through and the cheese melted.
11. Cut each pizza into 4 slices. Serve with the cauliflower "wings" on the side.

Nutrition Info:

- (Per serving) Calories: 360; Total fat: 20g; Saturated fat: 6.5g; Carbohydrates: 21g; Fiber: 2.5g; Protein: 24g; Sodium: 1,399mg

Bang-bang Chicken

Servings: 2
Cooking Time: 20 Minutes.
Ingredients:

- 1 cup mayonnaise
- ½ cup sweet chili sauce
- 2 tablespoons Sriracha sauce
- ⅓ cup flour
- 1 lb. boneless chicken breast, diced
- 1 ½ cups panko bread crumbs
- 2 green onions, chopped

Directions:

1. Mix mayonnaise with Sriracha and sweet chili sauce in a large bowl.
2. Keep ¾ cup of the mixture aside.
3. Add flour, chicken, breadcrumbs, and remaining mayo mixture to a resealable plastic bag.
4. Zip the bag and shake well to coat.
5. Divide the chicken in the two crisper plates in a single layer.
6. Return the crisper plate to the Ninja Foodi Dual Zone Air Fryer.
7. Choose the Air Fry mode for Zone 1 and set the temperature to 390 degrees F and the time to 20 minutes.
8. Select the "MATCH" button to copy the settings for Zone 2.
9. Initiate cooking by pressing the START/STOP button.
10. Flip the chicken once cooked halfway through.
11. Top the chicken with reserved mayo sauce.
12. Garnish with green onions and serve warm.

Nutrition Info:

- (Per serving) Calories 374 | Fat 13g | Sodium 552mg | Carbs 25g | Fiber 1.2g | Sugar 1.2g | Protein 37.7g

Pickled Chicken Fillets

Servings: 4
Cooking Time: 28 Minutes.

Ingredients:

- 2 boneless chicken breasts
- ½ cup dill pickle juice
- 2 eggs
- ½ cup milk
- 1 cup flour, all-purpose
- 2 tablespoons powdered sugar
- 2 tablespoons potato starch
- 1 teaspoon paprika
- 1 teaspoon of sea salt
- ½ teaspoon black pepper
- ½ teaspoon garlic powder
- ¼ teaspoon ground celery seed ground
- 1 tablespoon olive oil
- Cooking spray
- 4 hamburger buns, toasted
- 8 dill pickle chips

Directions:

1. Set the chicken in a suitable ziplock bag and pound it into ½ thickness with a mallet.
2. Slice the chicken into 2 halves.
3. Add pickle juice and seal the bag.
4. Refrigerate for 30 minutes approximately for marination. Whisk both eggs with milk in a shallow bowl.
5. Thoroughly mix flour with spices and flour in a separate bowl.
6. Dip each chicken slice in egg, then in the flour mixture.
7. Shake off the excess and set the chicken pieces in the crisper plate.
8. Spray the pieces with cooking oil.
9. Place the chicken pieces in the two crisper plate in a single layer and spray the cooking oil.
10. Return the crisper plate to the Ninja Foodi Dual Zone Air Fryer.
11. Choose the Air Fry mode for Zone 1 and set the temperature to 390 degrees F and the time to 28 minutes.
12. Select the "MATCH" button to copy the settings for Zone 2.
13. Initiate cooking by pressing the START/STOP button.
14. Flip the chicken pieces once cooked halfway through, and resume cooking.
15. Enjoy with pickle chips and a dollop of mayonnaise.

Nutrition Info:

- (Per serving) Calories 353 | Fat 5g | Sodium 818mg | Carbs 53.2g | Fiber 4.4g | Sugar 8g | Protein 17.3g

Spicy Chicken

Servings: 40
Cooking Time: 35

Ingredients:

- 4 chicken thighs
- 2 cups of butter milk
- 4 chicken legs
- 2 cups of flour
- Salt and black pepper, to taste
- 2 tablespoons garlic powder
- ½ teaspoon onion powder
- 1 teaspoon poultry seasoning
- 1 teaspoon cumin
- 2 tablespoons paprika
- 1 tablespoon olive oil

Directions:

1. Take a bowl and add buttermilk to it.
2. Soak the chicken thighs and chicken legs in the buttermilk for 2 hours.
3. Mix flour, all the seasonings, and olive oil in a small bowl.
4. Take out the chicken pieces from the buttermilk mixture and then dredge them into the flour mixture.
5. Repeat the steps for all the pieces and then arrange them into both the air fryer basket.
6. Set the timer for both the basket by selecting a roast mode for 35-40 minutes at 350 degrees F.
7. Once the cooking cycle complete select the pause button and then take out the basket.
8. Serve and enjoy.

Nutrition Info:

- (Per serving) Calories 624 | Fat 17.6 g | Sodium 300 mg | Carbs 60g | Fiber 3.5g | Sugar 7.7g | Protein 54.2 g

Fish And Seafood Recipes

Buttered Mahi-mahi

Servings: 4
Cooking Time: 22 Minutes.
Ingredients:
- 4 (6-oz) mahi-mahi fillets
- Salt and black pepper ground to taste
- Cooking spray
- ⅔ cup butter

Directions:
1. Preheat your Ninja Foodi Dual Zone Air Fryer to 350 degrees F.
2. Rub the mahi-mahi fillets with salt and black pepper.
3. Place two mahi-mahi fillets in each of the crisper plate.
4. Return the crisper plates to the Ninja Foodi Dual Zone Air Fryer.
5. Choose the Air Fry mode for Zone 1 and set the temperature to 390 degrees F and the time to 17 minutes.
6. Select the "MATCH" button to copy the settings for Zone 2.
7. Initiate cooking by pressing the START/STOP button.
8. Add butter to a saucepan and cook for 5 minutes until slightly brown.
9. Remove the butter from the heat.
10. Drizzle butter over the fish and serve warm.

Nutrition Info:
- (Per serving) Calories 399 | Fat 16g |Sodium 537mg | Carbs 28g | Fiber 3g | Sugar 10g | Protein 35g

Salmon With Green Beans

Servings:1
Cooking Time:18
Ingredients:
- 1 salmon fillet, 2 inches thick
- 2 teaspoons of olive oil
- 2 teaspoons of smoked paprika
- Salt and black pepper, to taste
- 1 cup green beans
- Oil spray, for greasing

Directions:
1. Grease the green beans with oil spray and add them to zone 1 basket.
2. Now rub the salmon fillet with olive oil, smoked paprika, salt, and black pepper.
3. Put the salmon fillets in the zone 2 basket.
4. Now set the zone one basket to AIRFRY mode at 350 degrees F for 18 minutes.
5. Set the Zone 2 basket to 390 degrees F for 16-18 minutes
6. Hit the smart finish button.
7. Once done, take out the salmon and green beans and transfer them to the serving plates and enjoy.

Nutrition Info:
- (Per serving) Calories 367| Fat22 g| Sodium 87mg | Carbs 10.2g | Fiber 5.3g | Sugar 2g | Protein 37.2g

Parmesan-crusted Fish Sticks With Baked Macaroni And Cheese

Servings: 4
Cooking Time: 25 Minutes

Ingredients:

- FOR THE FISH STICKS
- 1 pound cod or haddock fillets
- ½ cup all-purpose flour
- 2 large eggs
- ¼ teaspoon kosher salt
- ¼ teaspoon freshly ground black pepper
- ¾ cup panko bread crumbs
- ¼ cup grated Parmesan cheese
- Nonstick cooking spray

- FOR THE MACARONI AND CHEESE
- 1½ cups elbow macaroni
- 1 cup whole milk
- ½ cup heavy (whipping) cream
- 8 ounces shredded Colby-Jack cheese
- 4 ounces cream cheese, at room temperature
- 1 teaspoon Dijon mustard
- ½ teaspoon kosher salt
- ½ teaspoon freshly ground black pepper

Directions:

1. To prep the fish sticks: Cut the fish into sticks about 3 inches long and ¾ inch wide.
2. Set up a breading station with three small shallow bowls. Place the flour in the first bowl. In the second bowl, whisk the eggs and season with the salt and black pepper. Combine the panko and Parmesan in the third bowl.
3. Bread the fish sticks in this order: First, dip them into the flour, coating all sides. Then, dip into the beaten egg. Finally, coat them in the panko mixture, gently pressing the bread crumbs into the fish. Spritz each fish stick all over with cooking spray.
4. To prep the macaroni and cheese: Place the macaroni in the Zone 2 basket. Add the milk, cream, Colby-Jack, cream cheese, mustard, salt, and black pepper. Stir well to combine, ensuring the pasta is completely submerged in the liquid.
5. To cook the fish sticks and macaroni and cheese: Install a crisper plate in the Zone 1 basket. Arrange the fish sticks in a single layer in the basket (use a rack or cook in batches if necessary) and insert the basket in the unit. Insert the Zone 2 basket in the unit.
6. Select Zone 1, select AIR FRY, set the temperature to 390°F, and set the timer to 18 minutes.
7. Select Zone 2, select BAKE, set the temperature to 360°F, and set the timer to 25 minutes. Select SMART FINISH.
8. Press START/PAUSE to begin cooking.
9. When the Zone 1 timer reads 3 minutes, press START/PAUSE. Remove the basket and use silicone-tipped tongs to gently flip over the fish sticks. Reinsert the basket and press START/PAUSE to resume cooking.
10. When cooking is complete, the fish sticks should be crisp and the macaroni tender.
11. Stir the macaroni and cheese and let stand for 5 minutes before serving. The sauce will thicken as it cools.

Nutrition Info:

- (Per serving) Calories: 903; Total fat: 51g; Saturated fat: 25g; Carbohydrates: 60g; Fiber: 2.5g; Protein: 48g; Sodium: 844mg

Shrimp With Lemon And Pepper

Servings: 4
Cooking Time: 8 Minutes

Ingredients:

- 455g raw shrimp, peeled and deveined
- 118ml olive oil
- 2 tablespoons lemon juice
- 1 teaspoon black pepper
- ½ teaspoon salt

Directions:

1. Toss shrimp with black pepper, salt, lemon juice and oil in a bowl.
2. Divide the shrimp into the Ninja Foodi 2 Baskets Air Fryer baskets.
3. Return the air fryer basket 1 to Zone 1, and basket 2 to Zone 2 of the Ninja Foodi 2-Basket Air Fryer.
4. Choose the "Air Fry" mode for Zone 1 at 350 degrees F and 8 minutes of cooking time.
5. Select the "MATCH COOK" option to copy the settings for Zone 2.
6. Initiate cooking by pressing the START/PAUSE BUTTON.
7. Serve warm.

Nutrition Info:

- (Per serving) Calories 257 | Fat 10.4g | Sodium 431mg | Carbs 20g | Fiber 0g | Sugar 1.6g | Protein 21g

Frozen Breaded Fish Fillet

Servings: 2
Cooking Time: 12
Ingredients:
- 4 Frozen Breaded Fish Fillet
- Oil spray, for greasing
- 1 cup mayonnaise

Directions:
1. Take the frozen fish fillets out of the bag and place them in both baskets of the air fryer.
2. Lightly grease it with oil spray.
3. Set the Zone 1 basket to 380 degrees F fo12 minutes.
4. Select the MATCH button for the zone 2 basket.
5. hit the start button to start cooking.
6. Once the cooking is done, serve the fish hot with mayonnaise.

Nutrition Info:
- (Per serving) Calories 921| Fat 61.5g| Sodium 1575mg | Carbs 69g | Fiber 2g | Sugar 9.5g | Protein 29.1g

Blackened Mahimahi With Honey-roasted Carrots

Servings: 4
Cooking Time: 30 Minutes
Ingredients:
- FOR THE MAHIMAHI
- 4 mahimahi fillets (4 ounces each)
- 1 tablespoon olive oil
- 1 tablespoon blackening seasoning
- Lemon wedges, for serving
- FOR THE CARROTS
- 1 pound carrots, peeled and cut into ½-inch rounds
- 2 teaspoons vegetable oil
- ½ teaspoon kosher salt
- ¼ teaspoon freshly ground black pepper
- 1 tablespoon salted butter, cut into small pieces
- 1 tablespoon honey
- 2 tablespoons chopped fresh parsley

Directions:
1. To prep the mahimahi: Brush both sides of the fish with the oil and sprinkle with the blackening seasoning.
2. To prep the carrots: In a large bowl, combine the carrots, oil, salt, and black pepper. Stir well to coat the carrots with the oil.
3. To cook the mahimahi and carrots: Install a crisper plate in each of the two baskets. Place the fish in the Zone 1 basket and insert the basket in the unit. Place the carrots in the Zone 2 basket and insert the basket in the unit.
4. Select Zone 1, select AIR FRY, set the temperature to 380°F, and set the timer to 14 minutes.
5. Select Zone 2, select ROAST, set the temperature to 400°F, and set the timer to 30 minutes. Select SMART FINISH.
6. Press START/PAUSE to begin cooking.
7. When the Zone 2 timer reads 15 minutes, press START/PAUSE. Remove the basket and scatter the butter over the carrots, then drizzle them with the honey. Reinsert the basket and press START/PAUSE to resume cooking.
8. When cooking is complete, the fish should be cooked through and the carrots soft.
9. Stir the parsley into the carrots. Serve the fish with lemon wedges.

Nutrition Info:
- (Per serving) Calories: 235; Total fat: 9.5g; Saturated fat: 3g; Carbohydrates: 15g; Fiber: 3g; Protein: 22g; Sodium: 672mg

Flavorful Salmon With Green Beans

Servings: 4
Cooking Time: 10 Minutes
Ingredients:

- 4 ounces green beans
- 1 tablespoon canola oil
- 4 (6-ounce) salmon fillets
- 1/3 cup prepared sesame-ginger sauce
- Kosher salt, to taste
- Black pepper, to taste

Directions:
1. Toss the green beans with a teaspoon each of salt and pepper in a large bowl.
2. Place a crisper plate in each drawer. Place the green beans in the zone 1 drawer and insert it into the unit. Place the salmon into the zone 2 drawer and place it into the unit.
3. Select zone 1, then AIR FRY, and set the temperature to 390 degrees F/ 200 degrees C with a 10-minute timer.
4. Select zone 2, then AIR FRY, and set the temperature to 390 degrees F/ 200 degrees C with a 15-minute timer. Select SYNC. To begin cooking, press the START/STOP button.
5. Press START/STOP to pause the unit when the zone 2 timer reaches 9 minutes. Remove the salmon from the drawer and toss it in the sesame-ginger sauce. To resume cooking, replace the drawer in the device and press START/STOP.
6. When cooking is complete, serve the salmon and green beans immediately.

Nutrition Info:
- (Per serving) Calories 305 | Fat 16g | Sodium 535mg | Carbs 8.7g | Fiber 1g | Sugar 6.4g | Protein 34.9g

Spicy Salmon Fillets

Servings: 6
Cooking Time: 8 Minutes
Ingredients:

- 900g salmon fillets
- ¾ tsp ground cumin
- 1 tbsp brown sugar
- 2 tbsp steak seasoning
- ¼ tsp cayenne pepper
- ½ tsp ground coriander

Directions:
1. Mix ground cumin, coriander, steak seasoning, brown sugar, and cayenne in a small bowl.
2. Rub salmon fillets with spice mixture.
3. Insert a crisper plate in the Ninja Foodi air fryer baskets.
4. Place the salmon fillets in both baskets.
5. Select zone 1, then select "bake" mode and set the temperature to 360 degrees F for 10 minutes. Press "match" to match zone 2 settings to zone 1. Press "start/stop" to begin.

Nutrition Info:
- (Per serving) Calories 207 | Fat 9.4g | Sodium 68mg | Carbs 1.6g | Fiber 0.1g | Sugar 1.5g | Protein 29.4g

Shrimp Skewers

Servings: 4
Cooking Time: 10minutes
Ingredients:

- 453g shrimp
- 15ml lemon juice
- 15ml olive oil
- 1 tbsp old bay seasoning
- 1 tsp garlic, minced

Directions:
1. Toss shrimp with old bay seasoning, garlic, lemon juice, and olive oil in a bowl.
2. Thread shrimp onto the soaked skewers.
3. Insert a crisper plate in the Ninja Foodi air fryer baskets.
4. Place the shrimp skewers in both baskets.
5. Select zone 1, then select "air fry" mode and set the temperature to 390 degrees F for 10 minutes. Press "match" to match zone 2 settings to zone 1. Press "start/stop" to begin.

Nutrition Info:
- (Per serving) Calories 167 | Fat 5.5g | Sodium 758mg | Carbs 2g | Fiber 0g | Sugar 0.1g | Protein 25.9g

Crispy Fish Nuggets

Servings: 4
Cooking Time: 8 Minutes
Ingredients:
- 2 eggs
- 96g all-purpose flour
- 700g cod fish fillets, cut into pieces
- 1 tsp garlic powder
- 1 tbsp old bay seasoning
- Pepper
- Salt

Directions:
1. In a small bowl, whisk eggs.
2. Mix flour, garlic powder, old bay seasoning, pepper, and salt in a shallow dish.
3. Coat each fish piece with flour, then dip in egg and again coat with flour.
4. Insert a crisper plate in the Ninja Foodi air fryer baskets.
5. Place coated fish pieces in both baskets.
6. Select zone 1, then select "air fry" mode and set the temperature to 380 degrees F for 8 minutes. Press "match" to match zone 2 settings to zone 1. Press "start/stop" to begin.

Nutrition Info:
- (Per serving) Calories 298 | Fat 3.9g | Sodium 683mg | Carbs 18.6g | Fiber 0.7g | Sugar 0.4g | Protein 44.1g

Broiled Teriyaki Salmon With Eggplant In Stir-fry Sauce

Servings: 4
Cooking Time: 25 Minutes
Ingredients:
- FOR THE TERIYAKI SALMON
- 4 salmon fillets (6 ounces each)
- ½ cup teriyaki sauce
- 3 scallions, sliced
- FOR THE EGGPLANT
- ¼ cup reduced-sodium soy sauce
- ¼ cup packed light brown sugar
- 1 tablespoon minced fresh ginger
- 1 tablespoon minced garlic
- 2 teaspoons sesame oil
- ¼ teaspoon red pepper flakes
- 1 eggplant, peeled and cut into bite-size cubes
- Nonstick cooking spray

Directions:
1. To prep the teriyaki salmon: Brush the top of each salmon fillet with the teriyaki sauce.
2. To prep the eggplant: In a small bowl, whisk together the soy sauce, brown sugar, ginger, garlic, sesame oil, and red pepper flakes. Set the stir-fry sauce aside.
3. Spritz the eggplant cubes with cooking spray.
4. To cook the salmon and eggplant: Install a crisper plate in each of the two baskets. Place the salmon in a single layer in the Zone 1 basket and insert the basket in the unit. Place the eggplant in the Zone 2 basket and insert the basket in the unit.
5. Select Zone 1, select AIR BROIL, set the temperature to 450°F, and set the time to 8 minutes.
6. Select Zone 2, select AIR FRY, set the temperature to 390°F, and set the time to 25 minutes. Select SMART FINISH.
7. Press START/PAUSE to begin cooking.
8. When the Zone 2 timer reads 5 minutes, press START/PAUSE. Remove the basket and pour the stir-fry sauce evenly over the eggplant. Shake or stir to coat the eggplant cubes in the sauce. Reinsert the basket and press START/PAUSE to resume cooking.
9. When cooking is complete, the salmon should be cooked to your liking and the eggplant tender and slightly caramelized. Serve hot.

Nutrition Info:
- (Per serving) Calories: 499; Total fat: 22g; Saturated fat: 2g; Carbohydrates: 36g; Fiber: 3.5g; Protein: 42g; Sodium: 1,024mg

Crispy Parmesan Cod

Servings: 2
Cooking Time: 10 Minutes
Ingredients:
- 455g cod filets
- Salt and black pepper, to taste
- ½ cup flour
- 2 large eggs, beaten
- ½ teaspoon salt
- 1 cup Panko
- ½ cup grated parmesan
- 2 teaspoons old bay seasoning
- ½ teaspoon garlic powder
- Olive oil spray

Directions:
1. Rub the cod fillets with black pepper and salt.
2. Mix panko with parmesan cheese, old bay seasoning, and garlic powder in a bowl.
3. Mix flour with salt in another bowl.
4. Dredge the cod filets in the flour then dip in the eggs and coat with the Panko mixture.
5. Place the cod fillets in the air fryer baskets.
6. Return the air fryer basket 1 to Zone 1, and basket 2 to Zone 2 of the Ninja Foodi 2-Basket Air Fryer.
7. Choose the "Air Fry" mode for Zone 1 and set the temperature to 400 degrees F and 10 minutes of cooking time.
8. Select the "MATCH COOK" option to copy the settings for Zone 2.
9. Initiate cooking by pressing the START/PAUSE BUTTON.
10. Flip the cod fillets once cooked halfway through.
11. Serve warm.

Nutrition Info:
- (Per serving) Calories 275 | Fat 1.4g |Sodium 582mg | Carbs 31.5g | Fiber 1.1g | Sugar 0.1g | Protein 29.8g

Glazed Scallops

Servings: 6
Cooking Time: 13 Minutes.
Ingredients:
- 12 scallops
- 3 tablespoons olive oil
- Black pepper and salt to taste

Directions:
1. Rub the scallops with olive oil, black pepper, and salt.
2. Divide the scallops in the two crisper plates.
3. Return the crisper plate to the Ninja Foodi Dual Zone Air Fryer.
4. Choose the Air Fry mode for Zone 1 and set the temperature to 390 degrees F and the time to 13 minutes.
5. Select the "MATCH" button to copy the settings for Zone 2.
6. Initiate cooking by pressing the START/STOP button.
7. Flip the scallops once cooked halfway through, and resume cooking.
8. Serve warm.

Nutrition Info:
- (Per serving) Calories 308 | Fat 24g |Sodium 715mg | Carbs 0.8g | Fiber 0.1g | Sugar 0.1g | Protein 21.9g

Savory Salmon Fillets

Servings: 4
Cooking Time: 17 Minutes.

Ingredients:

- 4 (6-oz) salmon fillets
- Salt, to taste
- Black pepper, to taste
- 4 teaspoons olive oil
- 4 tablespoons wholegrain mustard
- 2 tablespoons packed brown sugar
- 2 garlic cloves, minced
- 1 teaspoon thyme leaves

Directions:

1. Rub the salmon with salt and black pepper first.
2. Whisk oil with sugar, thyme, garlic, and mustard in a small bowl.
3. Place two salmon fillets in each of the crisper plate and brush the thyme mixture on top of each fillet.
4. Return the crisper plates to the Ninja Foodi Dual Zone Air Fryer.
5. Choose the Air Fry mode for Zone 1 and set the temperature to 390 degrees F and the time to 17 minutes.
6. Select the "MATCH" button to copy the settings for Zone 2.
7. Initiate cooking by pressing the START/STOP button.
8. Serve warm and fresh.

Nutrition Info:

- (Per serving) Calories 336 | Fat 6g | Sodium 181mg | Carbs 1.3g | Fiber 0.2g | Sugar 0.4g | Protein 69.2g

"fried" Fish With Seasoned Potato Wedges

Servings:4
Cooking Time: 30 Minutes

Ingredients:

- FOR THE FISH
- 4 cod fillets (6 ounces each)
- 4 tablespoons all-purpose flour, divided
- ¼ cup cornstarch
- 1 teaspoon baking powder
- ¼ teaspoon kosher salt
- ⅓ cup lager-style beer or sparkling water
- Tartar sauce, cocktail sauce, or malt vinegar, for serving (optional)
- FOR THE POTATOES
- 4 russet potatoes
- 2 tablespoons vegetable oil
- ½ teaspoon paprika
- ½ teaspoon kosher salt
- ¼ teaspoon garlic powder
- ¼ teaspoon freshly ground black pepper

Directions:

1. To prep the fish: Pat the fish dry with a paper towel and coat lightly with 2 tablespoons of flour.
2. In a shallow dish, combine the remaining 2 tablespoons of flour, the cornstarch, baking powder, and salt. Stir in the beer to form a thick batter.
3. Dip the fish in the batter to coat both sides, then let rest on a cutting board for 10 minutes.
4. To prep the potatoes: Cut each potato in half lengthwise, then cut each half into 4 wedges.
5. In a large bowl, combine the potatoes and oil. Toss well to fully coat the potatoes. Add the paprika, salt, garlic powder, and black pepper and toss well to coat.
6. To cook the fish and potato wedges: Install a crisper plate in each of the two baskets. Place a piece of parchment paper or aluminum foil over the plate in the Zone 1 basket. Place the fish in the basket and insert the basket in the unit. Place the potato wedges in a single layer in the Zone 2 basket and insert the basket in the unit.
7. Select Zone 1, select AIR FRY, set the temperature to 400°F, and set the timer to 13 minutes.
8. Select Zone 2, select AIR FRY, set the temperature to 400°F, and set the timer to 30 minutes. Select SMART FINISH.
9. Press START/PAUSE to begin cooking.
10. When the Zone 1 timer reads 5 minutes, press START/PAUSE. Remove the basket and use a silicone spatula to carefully flip the fish over. Reinsert the basket and press START/PAUSE to resume cooking.
11. When cooking is complete, the fish should be cooked through and the potatoes crispy outside and tender inside. Serve hot with tartar sauce, cocktail sauce, or malt vinegar (if using).

Nutrition Info:

- (Per serving) Calories: 360; Total fat: 8g; Saturated fat: 1g; Carbohydrates: 40g; Fiber: 2g; Protein: 30g; Sodium: 302mg

Garlic Shrimp With Pasta Alfredo

Servings: 4
Cooking Time: 40 Minutes
Ingredients:
- FOR THE GARLIC SHRIMP
- 1 pound peeled small shrimp, thawed if frozen
- 1 tablespoon olive oil
- 1 tablespoon minced garlic
- ¼ teaspoon sea salt
- ¼ cup chopped fresh parsley
- FOR THE PASTA ALFREDO
- 8 ounces no-boil lasagna noodles
- 2 cups whole milk
- ¼ cup heavy (whipping) cream
- 2 tablespoons unsalted butter, cut into small pieces
- 1 tablespoon minced garlic
- ½ teaspoon kosher salt
- ¼ teaspoon freshly ground black pepper
- ½ cup grated Parmesan cheese

Directions:
1. To prep the garlic shrimp: In a large bowl, combine the shrimp, oil, garlic, and salt.
2. To prep the pasta alfredo: Break the lasagna noodles into 2-inch pieces. Add the milk to the Zone 2 basket, then add the noodles, cream, butter, garlic, salt, and black pepper. Stir well and ensure the pasta is fully submerged in the liquid.
3. To cook the shrimp and pasta: Install a crisper plate in the Zone 1 basket. Place the shrimp in the basket and insert the basket in the unit. Insert the Zone 2 basket in the unit.
4. Select Zone 1, select AIR FRY, set the temperature to 390°F, and set the timer to 13 minutes.
5. Select Zone 2, select BAKE, set the temperature to 360°F, and set the timer to 40 minutes. Select SMART FINISH.
6. Press START/PAUSE to begin cooking.
7. When the Zone 2 timer reads 20 minutes, press START/PAUSE. Remove the basket and stir the pasta. Reinsert the basket and press START/PAUSE to resume cooking.
8. When cooking is complete, the shrimp will be cooked through and the pasta tender.
9. Transfer the pasta to a serving dish and stir in the Parmesan. Top with the shrimp and parsley.

Nutrition Info:
- (Per serving) Calories: 542; Total fat: 23g; Saturated fat: 11g; Carbohydrates: 52g; Fiber: 2g; Protein: 34g; Sodium: 643mg

Fried Tilapia

Servings: 4
Cooking Time: 20 Minutes
Ingredients:
- 4 fresh tilapia fillets, approximately 6 ounces each
- 2 teaspoons olive oil
- 2 teaspoons chopped fresh chives
- 2 teaspoons chopped fresh parsley
- 1 teaspoon minced garlic
- Freshly ground pepper, to taste
- Salt to taste

Directions:
1. Pat the tilapia fillets dry with a paper towel.
2. Stir together the olive oil, chives, parsley, garlic, salt, and pepper in a small bowl.
3. Brush the mixture over the top of the tilapia fillets.
4. Place a crisper plate in each drawer. Add the fillets in a single layer to each drawer. Insert the drawers into the unit.
5. Select zone 1, then AIR FRY, then set the temperature to 360 degrees F/ 180 degrees C with a 20-minute timer. To match zone 2 settings to zone 1, choose MATCH. To begin, select START/STOP.
6. Remove the tilapia fillets from the drawers after the timer has finished.

Nutrition Info:
- (Per serving) Calories 140 | Fat 5.7g | Sodium 125mg | Carbs 1.5g | Fiber 0.4g | Sugar 0g | Protein 21.7g

Southwestern Fish Fillets

Servings: 4
Cooking Time: 16 Minutes
Ingredients:
- 455g trout fillets
- 1 tsp garlic powder
- 29g breadcrumbs
- 15ml olive oil
- 1 tsp chilli powder
- 1 tsp onion powder

Directions:
1. In a small bowl, mix breadcrumbs, garlic powder, onion powder, and chilli powder.
2. Brush fish fillets with oil and coat with breadcrumbs.
3. Insert a crisper plate in the Ninja Foodi air fryer baskets.
4. Place coated fish fillets in both baskets.
5. Select zone 1 then select "air fry" mode and set the temperature to 375 degrees F for 16 minutes. Press "match" and "start/stop" to begin.

Nutrition Info:
- (Per serving) Calories 272 | Fat 13.5g |Sodium 120mg | Carbs 5g | Fiber 0.6g | Sugar 0.7g | Protein 31.1g

Lemon Pepper Fish Fillets

Servings: 4
Cooking Time: 10 Minutes
Ingredients:
- 4 tilapia fillets
- 30ml olive oil
- 2 tbsp lemon zest
- ⅛ tsp paprika
- 1 tsp garlic, minced
- 1 ½ tsp ground peppercorns
- Pepper
- Salt

Directions:
1. In a small bowl, mix oil, peppercorns, paprika, garlic, lemon zest, pepper, and salt.
2. Brush the fish fillets with oil mixture.
3. Insert a crisper plate in the Ninja Foodi air fryer baskets.
4. Place fish fillets in both baskets.
5. Select zone 1 then select "air fry" mode and set the temperature to 390 degrees F for 10 minutes. Press "match" to match zone 2 settings to zone 1. Press "start/stop" to begin.

Nutrition Info:
- (Per serving) Calories 203 | Fat 9g |Sodium 99mg | Carbs 0.9g | Fiber 0.2g | Sugar 0.2g | Protein 32.1g

Tuna Patties

Servings: 6
Cooking Time: 10 Minutes
Ingredients:

- For the tuna patties:
- 1 tablespoon extra-virgin olive oil
- 1 tablespoon butter
- ½ cup chopped onion
- ½ red bell pepper, chopped
- 1 teaspoon minced garlic
- 2 (7-ounce) cans or 3 (5-ounce) cans albacore tuna fish in water, drained
- 1 tablespoon lime juice
- 1 celery stalk, chopped
- ¼ cup chopped fresh parsley
- 3 tablespoons grated parmesan cheese
- ½ teaspoon dried oregano
- ¼ teaspoon salt
- Black pepper, to taste
- 1 teaspoon sriracha
- ½ cup panko crumbs
- 2 whisked eggs
- For the crumb coating:
- ½ cup panko crumbs
- ¼ cup parmesan cheese
- Non-stick spray

Directions:
1. In a skillet, heat the oil and butter over medium-high heat.
2. Sauté the onions, red bell pepper, and garlic for 5 to 7 minutes.
3. Drain the tuna from the cans thoroughly. Put the tuna in a large mixing bowl. Add the lime juice.
4. Add the sautéed vegetables to the mixing bowl.
5. Add the celery, parsley, and cheese. Combine well.
6. Add the oregano, salt, and pepper to taste. Mix well.
7. Add a dash of sriracha for a spicy kick and mix well.
8. Add the panko crumbs and mix well.
9. Mix in the eggs until the mixture is well combined. You can add an extra egg if necessary, but the tuna is usually wet enough that it isn't required. Form 6 patties from the mixture.
10. Refrigerate for 30 to 60 minutes (or even overnight).
11. Remove from refrigerator and coat with a mixture of the ½ cup of panko crumbs and ¼ cup of parmesan cheese.
12. Spray the tops of the coated patties with some non-stick cooking spray.
13. Place a crisper place in each drawer. Put 3 patties in each drawer. Insert the drawers into the unit.
14. Select zone 1, then AIR FRY, then set the temperature to 390 degrees F/ 200 degrees C with a 10-minute timer. To match zone 2 settings to zone 1, choose MATCH. To begin, select START/STOP.
15. Remove and garnish with chopped parsley.

Nutrition Info:
- (Per serving) Calories 381 | Fat 16g | Sodium 1007mg | Carbs 23g | Fiber 2g | Sugar 4g | Protein 38g

Scallops

Servings: 4
Cooking Time: 5 Minutes
Ingredients:

- ½ cup Italian breadcrumbs
- ½ teaspoon garlic powder
- ¼ teaspoon salt
- ½ teaspoon black pepper
- 2 tablespoons butter, melted
- 1 pound sea scallops, rinsed and pat dry

Directions:
1. Combine the breadcrumbs, garlic powder, salt, and pepper in a small bowl. Pour the melted butter into another shallow bowl.
2. Dredge each scallop in the melted butter, then roll it in the breadcrumb mixture until well covered.
3. Place a crisper plate in each drawer. Put the scallops in a single layer in each drawer. Insert the drawers into the unit.
4. Select zone 1, then AIR FRY, then set the temperature to 360 degrees F/ 180 degrees C with a 5-minute timer. To match zone 2 settings to zone 1, choose MATCH. To begin, select START/STOP.
5. Press START/STOP to pause the unit when the timer reaches 3 minutes. Remove the drawers. Use tongs to carefully flip the scallops over. To resume cooking, re-insert the drawers into the unit and press START/STOP.
6. Remove the scallops from the drawers after the timer has finished.

Nutrition Info:
- (Per serving) Calories 81 | Fat 6g | Sodium 145mg | Carbs 3g | Fiber 4g | Sugar 1g | Protein 3g

Fish Tacos

Servings: 5
Cooking Time: 30 Minutes

Ingredients:
- 1 pound firm white fish such as cod, haddock, pollock, halibut, or walleye
- ¾ cup gluten-free flour blend
- 3 eggs
- 1 cup gluten-free panko breadcrumbs
- 1 teaspoon garlic powder
- 1 teaspoon onion powder
- 1 teaspoon cumin
- 1 teaspoon lemon pepper
- 1 teaspoon red chili flakes
- 1 teaspoon kosher salt, divided
- 1 teaspoon pepper, divided
- Cooking oil spray
- 1 package corn tortillas
- Toppings such as tomatoes, avocado, cabbage, radishes, jalapenos, salsa, or hot sauce (optional)

Directions:
1. Dry the fish with paper towels. (Make sure to thaw the fish if it's frozen.) Depending on the size of the fillets, cut the fish in half or thirds.
2. On both sides of the fish pieces, liberally season with salt and pepper.
3. Put the flour in a dish.
4. In a separate bowl, crack the eggs and whisk them together until well blended.
5. Put the panko breadcrumbs in another bowl. Add the garlic powder, onion powder, cumin, lemon pepper, and red chili flakes. Add salt and pepper to taste. Stir until everything is well blended.
6. Each piece of fish should be dipped in the flour, then the eggs, and finally in the breadcrumb mixture. Make sure that each piece is completely coated.
7. Put a crisper plate in each drawer. Arrange the fish pieces in a single layer in each drawer. Insert the drawers into the unit.
8. Select zone 1, then AIR FRY, then set the temperature to 360 degrees F/ 180 degrees C with a 20-minute timer. To match zone 2 settings to zone 1, choose MATCH. To begin, select START/STOP.
9. Remove the fish from the drawers after the timer has finished. Place the crispy fish on warmed tortillas.

Nutrition Info:
- (Per serving) Calories 534 | Fat 18g | Sodium 679mg | Carbs 63g | Fiber 8g | Sugar 3g | Protein 27g

Tilapia With Mojo And Crispy Plantains

Servings: 4
Cooking Time: 30 Minutes

Ingredients:
- FOR THE TILAPIA
- 4 tilapia fillets (6 ounces each)
- 2 tablespoons all-purpose flour
- Nonstick cooking spray
- ¼ cup freshly squeezed orange juice
- 3 tablespoons fresh lime juice
- 2 tablespoons olive oil
- 1 tablespoon minced garlic
- ½ teaspoon ground cumin
- ¼ teaspoon kosher salt
- FOR THE PLANTAINS
- 1 large green plantain
- 2 cups cold water
- 2 teaspoons kosher salt
- Nonstick cooking spray

Directions:
1. To prep the tilapia: Dust both sides of the tilapia fillets with the flour, then spritz with cooking spray.
2. In a small bowl, whisk together the orange juice, lime juice, oil, garlic, cumin, and salt. Set the mojo sauce aside.
3. To prep the plantains: Cut the ends from the plantain, then remove and discard the peel. Slice the plantain into 1-inch rounds.
4. In a large bowl, combine the water, salt, and plantains. Let soak for 15 minutes.
5. Drain the plantains and pat them dry with paper towels. Spray with cooking spray.
6. To cook the tilapia and plantains: Install a crisper plate in each of the two baskets. Place the tilapia in a single layer in the Zone 1 basket (work in batches if needed) and insert the basket in the unit. Place the plantains in the Zone 2 basket and insert the basket in the unit.
7. Select Zone 1, select AIR FRY, set the temperature to 390°F, and set the timer to 10 minutes.
8. Select Zone 2, select AIR FRY, set the temperature to 390°F, and set the timer to 30 minutes. Select SMART FINISH.
9. Press START/PAUSE to begin cooking.
10. When the Zone 2 timer reads 10 minutes, press START/PAUSE. Remove the basket and use silicone-tipped tongs to transfer the plantains, which should be tender, to a cutting board. Use the bottom of a heavy glass to smash each plantain flat. Spray both sides with cooking spray and place them back in the basket. Reinsert the basket and press START/PAUSE to resume cooking.
11. When the Zone 1 timer reads 5 minutes, press START/PAUSE. Remove the basket. Spoon half of the mojo sauce over the tilapia. Reinsert the basket and press START/PAUSE to resume cooking.
12. When cooking is complete, the fish should be cooked through and the plantains crispy. Serve the tilapia and plantains with the remaining mojo sauce for dipping.

Nutrition Info:
- (Per serving) Calories: 380; Total fat: 21g; Saturated fat: 2g; Carbohydrates: 20g; Fiber: 1g; Protein: 35g; Sodium: 217mg

Shrimp Po'boys With Sweet Potato Fries

Servings: 4
Cooking Time: 30 Minutes

Ingredients:
- FOR THE SHRIMP PO'BOYS
- ½ cup buttermilk
- 1 tablespoon Louisiana-style hot sauce
- ¾ cup all-purpose flour
- ½ cup cornmeal
- ½ teaspoon kosher salt
- ½ teaspoon paprika
- ½ teaspoon garlic powder
- ½ teaspoon freshly ground black pepper
- 1 pound peeled medium shrimp, thawed if frozen
- Nonstock cooking spray
- ½ cup store-bought rémoulade sauce
- 4 French bread rolls, halved lengthwise
- ½ cup shredded lettuce
- 1 tomato, sliced
- FOR THE SWEET POTATO FRIES
- 2 medium sweet potatoes
- 2 teaspoons vegetable oil
- ¼ teaspoon garlic powder
- ¼ teaspoon paprika
- ¼ teaspoon kosher salt

Directions:
1. To prep the shrimp: In a medium bowl, combine the buttermilk and hot sauce. In a shallow bowl, combine the flour, cornmeal, salt, paprika, garlic powder, and black pepper.
2. Add the shrimp to the buttermilk and stir to coat. Remove the shrimp, letting the excess buttermilk drip off, then add to the cornmeal mixture to coat.
3. Spritz the breaded shrimp with cooking spray, then let sit for 10 minutes.
4. To prep the sweet potatoes: Peel the sweet potatoes and cut them lengthwise into ¼-inch-thick sticks (like shoestring fries).
5. In a large bowl, combine the sweet potatoes, oil, garlic powder, paprika, and salt. Toss to coat.
6. To cook the shrimp and fries: Install a crisper plate in each of the two baskets. Place the shrimp in the Zone 1 basket and insert the basket in the unit. Place the sweet potatoes in a single layer in the Zone 2 basket and insert the basket in the unit.
7. Select Zone 1, select AIR FRY, set the temperature to 390°F, and set the timer to 13 minutes.
8. Select Zone 2, select AIR FRY, set the temperature to 400°F, and set the timer to 30 minutes. Select SMART FINISH.
9. Press START/PAUSE to begin cooking.
10. When cooking is complete, the shrimp should be golden and cooked through and the sweet potato fries crisp.
11. Spread the rémoulade on the cut sides of the rolls. Divide the lettuce and tomato among the rolls, then top with the fried shrimp. Serve with the sweet potato fries on the side.

Nutrition Info:
- (Per serving) Calories: 669; Total fat: 22g; Saturated fat: 2g; Carbohydrates: 86g; Fiber: 3.5g; Protein: 33g; Sodium: 1,020mg

Vegetables And Sides Recipes

Garlic Potato Wedges In Air Fryer

Servings:2
Cooking Time:23

Ingredients:
- 4 medium potatoes, peeled and cut into wedges
- 4 tablespoons of butter
- 1 teaspoon of chopped cilantro
- 1 cup plain flour
- 1 teaspoon of garlic, minced
- Salt and black pepper, to taste

Directions:
1. Soak the potatoes wedges in cold water for about 30 minutes.
2. Then drain and pat dry with a paper towel.
3. Boil water in a large pot and boil the wedges just for 3 minutes.
4. Then take it out on a paper towel.
5. Now in a bowl mix garlic, melted butter, salt, pepper, cilantro and whisk it well.
6. Add the flour to a separate bowl and add salt and black pepper.
7. Then add water to the flour so it gets runny in texture.
8. Now, coat the potatoes with flour mixture and add it to two foil tins.
9. Put foil tins in both the air fryer basket.
10. Now, set time for zone 1 basket using AIRFRY mode at 390 degrees F for 20 minutes.
11. Select the MATCH button for the zone 2 basket.
12. Once done, serve and enjoy.

Nutrition Info:
- (Per serving) Calories 727| Fat 24.1g| Sodium 191mg | Carbs 115.1g | Fiber 12g | Sugar 5.1g | Protein14 g

Green Tomato Stacks

Servings: 6
Cooking Time: 12 Minutes

Ingredients:
- ¼ cup mayonnaise
- ¼ teaspoon lime zest, grated
- 2 tablespoons lime juice
- 1 teaspoon minced fresh thyme
- ½ teaspoon black pepper
- ¼ cup all-purpose flour
- 2 large egg whites, beaten
- ¾ cup cornmeal
- ¼ teaspoon salt
- 2 medium green tomatoes
- 2 medium re tomatoes
- Cooking spray
- 8 slices Canadian bacon, warmed

Directions:
1. Mix mayonnaise with ¼ teaspoon black pepper, thyme, lime juice and zest in a bowl.
2. Spread flour in one bowl, beat egg whites in another bowl and mix cornmeal with ¼ teaspoon black pepper and salt in a third bowl.
3. Cut the tomatoes into 4 slices and coat each with the flour then dip in the egg whites.
4. Coat the tomatoes slices with the cornmeal mixture.
5. Place the slices in the air fryer baskets.
6. Return the air fryer basket 1 to Zone 1, and basket 2 to Zone 2 of the Ninja Foodi 2-Basket Air Fryer.
7. Choose the "Air Fry" mode for Zone 1 at 390 degrees F and 12 minutes of cooking time.
8. Select the "MATCH COOK" option to copy the settings for Zone 2.
9. Initiate cooking by pressing the START/PAUSE BUTTON.
10. Flip the tomatoes once cooked halfway through.
11. Place the green tomato slices on the working surface.
12. Top them with bacon, and red tomato slice.
13. Serve.

Nutrition Info:
- (Per serving) Calories 113 | Fat 3g |Sodium 152mg | Carbs 20g | Fiber 3g | Sugar 1.1g | Protein 3.5g

Veggie Burgers With "fried" Onion Rings

Servings: 4
Cooking Time: 25 Minutes

Ingredients:
- FOR THE VEGGIE BURGERS
- 1 (15-ounce) can black beans, drained and rinsed
- ½ cup panko bread crumbs
- 1 large egg
- ¼ cup finely chopped red bell pepper
- ¼ cup frozen corn, thawed
- 1 tablespoon olive oil
- ½ teaspoon garlic powder
- ½ teaspoon ground cumin
- ¼ teaspoon smoked paprika
- Nonstick cooking spray
- 4 hamburger buns
- ¼ cup barbecue sauce, for serving
- FOR THE ONION RINGS
- 1 large sweet onion
- ½ cup all-purpose flour
- 2 large eggs
- 1 cup panko bread crumbs
- ½ teaspoon kosher salt
- Nonstick cooking spray

Directions:
1. To prep the veggie burgers: In a large bowl, mash the beans with a potato masher or a fork. Stir in the panko, egg, bell pepper, corn, oil, garlic powder, cumin, and smoked paprika. Mix well.
2. Shape the mixture into 4 patties. Spritz both sides of each patty with cooking spray.
3. To prep the onion rings: Cut the onion into ½-inch-thick rings.
4. Set up a breading station with three small shallow bowls. Place the flour in the first bowl. In the second bowl, beat the eggs. Place the panko and salt in the third bowl.
5. Bread the onions rings in this order: First, dip them into the flour, coating both sides. Then, dip into the beaten egg. Finally, coat them in the panko. Spritz each with cooking spray.
6. To cook the burgers and onion rings: Install a crisper plate in each of the two baskets. Place 2 veggie burgers in the Zone 1 basket. Place the onion rings in the Zone 2 basket and insert both baskets in the unit.
7. Select Zone 1, select AIR FRY, set the temperature to 390°F, and set the timer to 25 minutes.
8. Select Zone 2, select AIR FRY, set the temperature to 375°F, and set the timer to 10 minutes. Select SMART FINISH.
9. Press START/PAUSE to begin cooking.
10. When the Zone 1 timer reads 10 minutes, press START/PAUSE. Remove the basket and use a silicone spatula to flip the burgers. Reinsert the basket and press START/PAUSE to resume cooking.
11. When the Zone 1 timer reads 10 minutes, press START/PAUSE. Remove the basket and transfer the burgers to a plate. Place the 2 remaining burgers in the basket. Reinsert the basket and press START/PAUSE to resume cooking.
12. When both timers read 5 minutes, press START/PAUSE. Remove the Zone 1 basket and flip the burgers, then reinsert the basket. Remove the Zone 2 basket and shake vigorously to rearrange the onion rings and separate any that have stuck together. Reinsert the basket and press START/PAUSE to resume cooking.
13. When cooking is complete, the veggie burgers should be cooked through and the onion rings golden brown.
14. Place 1 burger on each bun. Top with barbecue sauce and serve with onion rings on the side.

Nutrition Info:
- (Per serving) Calories: 538; Total fat: 16g; Saturated fat: 2g; Carbohydrates: 83g; Fiber: 10g; Protein: 19g; Sodium: 914mg

Fried Artichoke Hearts

Servings: 6
Cooking Time: 10 Minutes.

Ingredients:
- 3 cans Quartered Artichokes, drained
- ½ cup mayonnaise
- 1 cup panko breadcrumbs
- ⅓ cup grated Parmesan
- salt and black pepper to taste
- Parsley for garnish

Directions:
1. Mix mayonnaise with salt and black pepper and keep the sauce aside.
2. Spread panko breadcrumbs in a bowl.
3. Coat the artichoke pieces with the breadcrumbs.
4. As you coat the artichokes, place them in the two crisper plates in a single layer, then spray them with cooking oil.
5. Return the crisper plates to the Ninja Foodi Dual Zone Air Fryer.
6. Choose the Air Fry mode for Zone 1 and set the temperature to 375 degrees F and the time to 10 minutes.
7. Select the "MATCH" button to copy the settings for Zone 2.
8. Initiate cooking by pressing the START/STOP button.
9. Flip the artichokes once cooked halfway through, then resume cooking.
10. Serve warm with mayo sauce.

Nutrition Info:
- (Per serving) Calories 193 | Fat 1g |Sodium 395mg | Carbs 38.7g | Fiber 1.6g | Sugar 0.9g | Protein 6.6g

Green Salad With Crispy Fried Goat Cheese And Baked Croutons

Servings:4
Cooking Time: 10 Minutes

Ingredients:
- FOR THE GOAT CHEESE
- 1 (4-ounce) log soft goat cheese
- ½ cup panko bread crumbs
- 2 tablespoons vegetable oil
- FOR THE CROUTONS
- 2 slices Italian-style sandwich bread
- 2 tablespoons vegetable oil
- 1 tablespoon poultry seasoning
- ½ teaspoon kosher salt
- ¼ teaspoon freshly ground black pepper
- FOR THE SALAD
- 8 cups green leaf lettuce leaves
- ½ cup store-bought balsamic vinaigrette

Directions:
1. To prep the goat cheese: Cut the goat cheese into 8 round slices.
2. Spread the panko on a plate. Gently press the cheese into the panko to coat on both sides. Drizzle with the oil.
3. To prep the croutons: Cut the bread into cubes and place them in a large bowl. Add the oil, poultry seasoning, salt, and black pepper. Mix well to coat the bread cubes evenly.
4. To cook the goat cheese and croutons: Install a crisper plate in each of the two baskets. Place the goat cheese in the Zone 1 basket and insert the basket in the unit. Place the croutons in the Zone 2 basket and insert the basket in the unit.
5. Select Zone 1, select AIR FRY, set the temperature to 400°F, and set the timer to 6 minutes.
6. Select Zone 2, select BAKE, set the temperature to 390°F, and set the timer to 10 minutes. Select SMART FINISH.
7. Press START/PAUSE to begin cooking.
8. When cooking is complete, the goat cheese will be golden brown and the croutons crisp.
9. Remove the Zone 1 basket. Let the goat cheese cool in the basket for 5 minutes; it will firm up as it cools.
10. To assemble the salad: In a large bowl, combine the lettuce, vinaigrette, and croutons. Toss well. Divide the salad among four plates. Top each plate with 2 pieces of goat cheese.

Nutrition Info:
- (Per serving) Calories: 578; Total fat: 40g; Saturated fat: 14g; Carbohydrates: 39g; Fiber: 3.5g; Protein: 24g; Sodium: 815mg

Buffalo Seitan With Crispy Zucchini Noodles

Servings: 4
Cooking Time: 12 Minutes

Ingredients:
- FOR THE BUFFALO SEITAN
- 1 (8-ounce) package precooked seitan strips
- 1 teaspoon garlic powder, divided
- ½ teaspoon onion powder
- ¼ teaspoon smoked paprika
- ¼ cup Louisiana-style hot sauce
- 2 tablespoons vegetable oil
- 1 tablespoon tomato paste
- ¼ teaspoon freshly ground black pepper
- FOR THE ZUCCHINI NOODLES
- 3 large egg whites
- 1¼ cups all-purpose flour
- 1 teaspoon kosher salt, divided
- 12 ounces seltzer water or club soda
- 5 ounces zucchini noodles
- Nonstick cooking spray

Directions:
1. To prep the Buffalo seitan: Season the seitan strips with ½ teaspoon of garlic powder, the onion powder, and smoked paprika.
2. In a large bowl, whisk together the hot sauce, oil, tomato paste, remaining ½ teaspoon of garlic powder, and the black pepper. Set the bowl of Buffalo sauce aside.
3. To prep the zucchini noodles: In a medium bowl, use a handheld mixer to beat the egg whites until stiff peaks form.
4. In a large bowl, combine the flour and ½ teaspoon of salt. Mix in the seltzer to form a thin batter. Fold in the beaten egg whites.
5. Add the zucchini to the batter and gently mix to coat.
6. To cook the seitan and zucchini noodles: Install a crisper plate in each of the two baskets. Place the seitan in the Zone 1 basket and insert the basket in the unit. Lift the noodles from the batter one at a time, letting the excess drip off, and place them in the Zone 2 basket. Insert the basket in the unit.
7. Select Zone 1, select BAKE, set the temperature to 370°F, and set the timer to 12 minutes.
8. Select Zone 2, select AIR FRY, set the temperature to 400°F, and set the timer to 12 minutes. Select SMART FINISH.
9. Press START/PAUSE to begin cooking.
10. When the Zone 1 timer reads 2 minutes, press START/PAUSE. Remove the basket and transfer the seitan to the bowl of Buffalo sauce. Turn to coat, then return the seitan to the basket. Reinsert the basket and press START/PAUSE to resume cooking.
11. When cooking is complete, the seitan should be warmed through and the zucchini noodles crisp and light golden brown.
12. Sprinkle the zucchini noodles with the remaining ½ teaspoon of salt. If desired, drizzle extra Buffalo sauce over the seitan. Serve hot.

Nutrition Info:
- (Per serving) Calories: 252; Total fat: 15g; Saturated fat: 1g; Carbohydrates: 22g; Fiber: 1.5g; Protein: 13g; Sodium: 740mg

Acorn Squash Slices

Servings: 6
Cooking Time: 10 Minutes

Ingredients:
- 2 medium acorn squashes
- ⅔ cup packed brown sugar
- ½ cup butter, melted

Directions:
1. Cut the squash in half, remove the seeds and slice into ½ inch slices.
2. Place the squash slices in the air fryer baskets.
3. Drizzle brown sugar and butter over the squash slices.
4. Return the air fryer basket 1 to Zone 1, and basket 2 to Zone 2 of the Ninja Foodi 2-Basket Air Fryer.
5. Choose the "Air Fry" mode for Zone 1 and set the temperature to 350 degrees F and 10 minutes of cooking time.
6. Select the "MATCH COOK" option to copy the settings for Zone 2.
7. Initiate cooking by pressing the START/PAUSE BUTTON.
8. Flip the squash once cooked halfway through.
9. Serve.

Nutrition Info:
- (Per serving) Calories 206 | Fat 3.4g | Sodium 174mg | Carbs 35g | Fiber 9.4g | Sugar 5.9g | Protein 10.6g

Cheesy Potatoes With Asparagus

Servings: 2
Cooking Time: 35

Ingredients:
- 1-1/2 pounds of russet potato, wedges or cut in half
- 2 teaspoons mixed herbs
- 2 teaspoons chili flakes
- 2 cups asparagus
- 1 cup chopped onion
- 1 tablespoon Dijon mustard
- 1/4 cup fresh cream
- 1 teaspoon olive oil
- 2 tablespoons of butter
- 1/2 teaspoon salt and black pepper
- Water as required
- 1/2 cup Parmesan cheese

Directions:
1. Take a bowl and add asparagus and sweet potato wedges to it.
2. Season it with salt, black pepper, and olive oil.
3. Now add the potato wedges to the zone 1 air fryer basket and asparagus to the zone 2 basket.
4. Set basket1 to AIRFRY mode at 390 degrees F for 12 minutes.
5. Set the zone 2 basket at 390 degrees F, for 30-35 minutes.
6. Meanwhile, take a skillet and add butter and sauté onion in it for a few minutes.
7. Then add salt and Dijon mustard and chili flakes, Parmesan cheese, and fresh cream.
8. Once the air fry mode is done, take out the potato and asparagus.
9. Drizzle the skillet ingredients over the potatoes and serve with asparagus.

Nutrition Info:
- (Per serving) Calories 251| Fat11g | Sodium 279mg | Carbs 31.1g | Fiber 5g | Sugar 4.1g | Protein9 g

Lemon Herb Cauliflower

Servings: 4
Cooking Time: 10 Minutes

Ingredients:
- 384g cauliflower florets
- 1 tsp lemon zest, grated
- 1 tbsp thyme, minced
- 60ml olive oil
- 1 tbsp rosemary, minced
- ¼ tsp red pepper flakes, crushed
- 30ml lemon juice
- 25g parsley, minced
- ½ tsp salt

Directions:
1. In a bowl, toss cauliflower florets with the remaining ingredients until well coated.
2. Insert a crisper plate in the Ninja Foodi air fryer baskets.
3. Add cauliflower florets into both baskets.
4. Select zone 1, then select "air fry" mode and set the temperature to 360 degrees F for 10 minutes. Press "match" and "start/stop" to begin.

Nutrition Info:
- (Per serving) Calories 166 | Fat 14.4g |Sodium 340mg | Carbs 9.5g | Fiber 4.6g | Sugar 3.8g | Protein 3.3g

Falafel

Servings: 6
Cooking Time: 14 Minutes.

Ingredients:

- 1 (15.5-oz) can chickpeas, rinsed and drained
- 1 small yellow onion, cut into quarters
- 3 garlic cloves, chopped
- ⅓ cup parsley, chopped
- ⅓ cup cilantro, chopped
- ⅓ cup scallions, chopped
- 1 teaspoon cumin
- ½ teaspoons salt
- ⅛ teaspoons crushed red pepper flakes
- 1 teaspoon baking powder
- 4 tablespoons all-purpose flour
- Olive oil spray

Directions:

1. Dry the chickpeas on paper towels.
2. Add onions and garlic to a food processor and chop them.
3. Add the parsley, salt, cilantro, scallions, cumin, and red pepper flakes.
4. Press the pulse button for 60 seconds, then toss in chickpeas and blend for 3 times until it makes a chunky paste.
5. Stir in baking powder and flour and mix well.
6. Transfer the falafel mixture to a bowl and cover to refrigerate for 3 hours.
7. Make 12 balls out of the falafel mixture.
8. Place 6 falafels in each of the crisper plate and spray them with oil.
9. Return the crisper plate to the Ninja Foodi Dual Zone Air Fryer.
10. Choose the Air Fry mode for Zone 1 and set the temperature to 350 degrees F and the time to 14 minutes.
11. Select the "MATCH" button to copy the settings for Zone 2.
12. Initiate cooking by pressing the START/STOP button.
13. Toss the falafel once cooked halfway through, and resume cooking.
14. Serve warm.

Nutrition Info:

- (Per serving) Calories 113 | Fat 3g |Sodium 152mg | Carbs 20g | Fiber 3g | Sugar 1.1g | Protein 3.5g

Green Beans With Baked Potatoes

Servings:2
Cooking Time:45

Ingredients:

- 2 cups of green beans
- 2 large potatoes, cubed
- 3 tablespoons of olive oil
- 1 teaspoon of seasoned salt
- ½ teaspoon chili powder
- 1/6 teaspoon garlic powder
- 1/4 teaspoon onion powder

Directions:

1. Take a large bowl and pour olive oil into it.
2. Now add all the seasoning in the olive oil and whisk it well.
3. Toss the green bean in it, then transfer it to zone 1 basket of the air fryer.
4. Now season the potatoes with the seasoning and add them to the zone 2 basket.
5. Now set the zone one basket to AIRFRY mode at 350 degrees F for 18 minutes.
6. Now hit 2 for the second basket and set it to AIR FRY mode at 350 degrees F, for 45 minutes.
7. Once the cooking cycle is complete, take out and serve it by transferring it to the serving plates.

Nutrition Info:

- (Per serving) Calories473 | Fat21.6g | Sodium796 mg | Carbs 66.6g | Fiber12.9 g | Sugar6 g | Protein8.4 g

Lime Glazed Tofu

Servings: 6
Cooking Time: 14 Minutes.

Ingredients:
- ⅔ cup coconut aminos
- 2 (14-oz) packages extra-firm, water-packed tofu, drained
- 6 tablespoons toasted sesame oil
- ⅔ cup lime juice

Directions:
1. Pat dry the tofu bars and slice into half-inch cubes.
2. Toss all the remaining ingredients in a small bowl.
3. Marinate for 4 hours in the refrigerator. Drain off the excess water.
4. Divide the tofu cubes in the two crisper plates.
5. Return the crisper plates to the Ninja Foodi Dual Zone Air Fryer.
6. Choose the Air Fry mode for Zone 1 and set the temperature to 400 degrees F and the time to 14 minutes.
7. Select the "MATCH" button to copy the settings for Zone 2.
8. Initiate cooking by pressing the START/STOP button.
9. Toss the tofu once cooked halfway through, then resume cooking.
10. Serve warm.

Nutrition Info:
- (Per serving) Calories 284 | Fat 7.9g | Sodium 704mg | Carbs 38.1g | Fiber 1.9g | Sugar 1.9g | Protein 14.8g

Chickpea Fritters

Servings: 6
Cooking Time: 6 Minutes

Ingredients:
- 237ml plain yogurt
- 2 tablespoons sugar
- 1 tablespoon honey
- ½ teaspoon salt
- ½ teaspoon black pepper
- ½ teaspoon crushed red pepper flakes
- 1 can (28g) chickpeas, drained
- 1 teaspoon ground cumin
- ½ teaspoon salt
- ½ teaspoon garlic powder
- ½ teaspoon ground ginger
- 1 large egg
- ½ teaspoon baking soda
- ½ cup fresh coriander, chopped
- 2 green onions, sliced

Directions:
1. Mash chickpeas with rest of the ingredients in a food processor.
2. Layer the two air fryer baskets with a parchment paper.
3. Drop the batter in the baskets spoon by spoon.
4. Return the air fryer basket 1 to Zone 1, and basket 2 to Zone 2 of the Ninja Foodi 2-Basket Air Fryer.
5. Choose the "Air Fry" mode for Zone 1 at 400 degrees F and 6 minutes of cooking time.
6. Select the "MATCH COOK" option to copy the settings for Zone 2.
7. Initiate cooking by pressing the START/PAUSE BUTTON.
8. Flip the fritters once cooked halfway through.
9. Serve warm.

Nutrition Info:
- (Per serving) Calories 284 | Fat 7.9g | Sodium 704mg | Carbs 38.1g | Fiber 1.9g | Sugar 1.9g | Protein 14.8g

Bacon Wrapped Corn Cob

Servings: 4
Cooking Time: 10 Minutes
Ingredients:
- 4 trimmed corns on the cob
- 8 bacon slices

Directions:
1. Wrap the corn cobs with two bacon slices.
2. Place the wrapped cobs into the Ninja Foodi 2 Baskets Air Fryer baskets.
3. Return the air fryer basket 1 to Zone 1, and basket 2 to Zone 2 of the Ninja Foodi 2-Basket Air Fryer.
4. Choose the "Air Fry" mode for Zone 1 and set the temperature to 355 degrees F and 10 minutes of cooking time.
5. Select the "MATCH COOK" option to copy the settings for Zone 2.
6. Initiate cooking by pressing the START/PAUSE BUTTON.
7. Flip the corn cob once cooked halfway through.
8. Serve warm.

Nutrition Info:
- (Per serving) Calories 350 | Fat 2.6g |Sodium 358mg | Carbs 64.6g | Fiber 14.4g | Sugar 3.3g | Protein 19.9g

Air-fried Radishes

Servings: 6
Cooking Time: 15 Minutes
Ingredients:
- 1020g radishes, quartered
- 3 tablespoons olive oil
- 1 tablespoon fresh oregano, minced
- ¼ teaspoon salt
- ⅛ teaspoon black pepper

Directions:
1. Toss radishes with oil, black pepper, salt and oregano in a bowl.
2. Divide the radishes into the Ninja Foodi 2 Baskets Air Fryer baskets.
3. Return the air fryer basket 1 to Zone 1, and basket 2 to Zone 2 of the Ninja Foodi 2-Basket Air Fryer.
4. Choose the "Air Fry" mode for Zone 1 at 375 degrees F and 15 minutes of cooking time.
5. Select the "MATCH COOK" option to copy the settings for Zone 2.
6. Initiate cooking by pressing the START/PAUSE BUTTON.
7. Toss the radishes once cooked halfway through.
8. Serve.

Nutrition Info:
- (Per serving) Calories 270 | Fat 14.6g |Sodium 394mg | Carbs 31.3g | Fiber 7.5g | Sugar 9.7g | Protein 6.4g

Potatoes & Beans

Servings: 4
Cooking Time: 25 Minutes
Ingredients:
- 453g potatoes, cut into pieces
- 15ml olive oil
- 1 tsp garlic powder
- 160g green beans, trimmed
- Pepper
- Salt

Directions:
1. In a bowl, toss green beans, garlic powder, potatoes, oil, pepper, and salt.
2. Insert a crisper plate in the Ninja Foodi air fryer baskets.
3. Add green beans and potato mixture to both baskets.
4. Select zone 1 then select "air fry" mode and set the temperature to 380 degrees F for 25 minutes. Press "match" to match zone 2 settings to zone 1. Press "start/stop" to begin. Stir halfway through.

Nutrition Info:
- (Per serving) Calories 128 | Fat 3.7g |Sodium 49mg | Carbs 22.4g | Fiber 4.7g | Sugar 2.3g | Protein 3.1g

Hasselback Potatoes

Servings: 4
Cooking Time: 15 Minutes.

Ingredients:

- 4 medium Yukon Gold potatoes
- 3 tablespoons melted butter
- 1 tablespoon olive oil
- 3 garlic cloves, crushed
- ½ teaspoon ground paprika
- Salt and black pepper ground, to taste
- 1 tablespoon chopped fresh parsley

Directions:

1. Slice each potato from the top to make ¼-inch slices without cutting its ½-inch bottom, keeping the potato's bottom intact.
2. Mix butter with olive oil, garlic, and paprika in a small bowl.
3. Brush the garlic mixture on top of each potato and add the mixture into the slits.
4. Season them with salt and black pepper.
5. Place 2 seasoned potatoes in each of the crisper plate
6. Return the crisper plate to the Ninja Foodi Dual Zone Air Fryer.
7. Choose the Air Fry mode for Zone 1 and set the temperature to 375 degrees F and the time to 25 minutes.
8. Select the "MATCH" button to copy the settings for Zone 2.
9. Initiate cooking by pressing the START/STOP button.
10. Brushing the potatoes again with butter mixture after 15 minutes, then resume cooking.
11. Garnish with parsley.
12. Serve warm.

Nutrition Info:

- (Per serving) Calories 350 | Fat 2.6g | Sodium 358mg | Carbs 64.6g | Fiber 14.4g | Sugar 3.3g | Protein 19.9g

Broccoli, Squash, & Pepper

Servings: 4
Cooking Time: 12 Minutes

Ingredients:

- 175g broccoli florets
- 1 red bell pepper, diced
- 1 tbsp olive oil
- ½ tsp garlic powder
- ¼ onion, sliced
- 1 zucchini, sliced
- 2 yellow squash, sliced
- Pepper
- Salt

Directions:

1. In a bowl, toss veggies with oil, garlic powder, pepper, and salt.
2. Insert a crisper plate in the Ninja Foodi air fryer baskets.
3. Add the vegetable mixture in both baskets.
4. Select zone 1 then select "air fry" mode and set the temperature to 390 degrees F for 12 minutes. Press "match" to match zone 2 settings to zone 1. Press "start/stop" to begin. Stir halfway through.

Nutrition Info:

- (Per serving) Calories 75 | Fat 3.9g | Sodium 62mg | Carbs 9.6g | Fiber 2.8g | Sugar 4.8g | Protein 2.9g

Kale And Spinach Chips

Servings: 2
Cooking Time: 6

Ingredients:

- 2 cups spinach, torn in pieces and stem removed
- 2 cups kale, torn in pieces, stems removed
- 1 tablespoon of olive oil
- Sea salt, to taste
- 1/3 cup Parmesan cheese

Directions:

1. Take a bowl and add spinach to it.
2. Take another bowl and add kale to it.
3. Now, season both of them with olive oil, and sea salt.
4. Add kale to zone 1 basket and spinach to zone 2 basket.
5. Select the zone 1 air fry mode at 350 degrees F for 6 minutes.
6. Set zone 2 to AIR FRY mode at 350 for 5 minutes.
7. Once done, take out the crispy chips and sprinkle Parmesan cheese on top.
8. Serve and Enjoy.

Nutrition Info:

- (Per serving) Calories 166| Fat 11.1g| Sodium 355mg | Carbs 8.1g | Fiber1.7 g | Sugar 0.1g | Protein 8.2g

Fried Olives

Servings: 6
Cooking Time: 9 Minutes.

Ingredients:

- 2 cups blue cheese stuffed olives, drained
- ½ cup all-purpose flour
- 1 cup panko breadcrumbs
- ½ teaspoon garlic powder
- 1 pinch oregano
- 2 eggs

Directions:

1. Mix flour with oregano and garlic powder in a bowl and beat two eggs in another bowl.
2. Spread panko breadcrumbs in a bowl.
3. Coat all the olives with the flour mixture, dip in the eggs and then coat with the panko breadcrumbs.
4. As you coat the olives, place them in the two crisper plates in a single layer, then spray them with cooking oil.
5. Return the crisper plates to the Ninja Foodi Dual Zone Air Fryer.
6. Choose the Air Fry mode for Zone 1 and set the temperature to 375 degrees F and the time to 9 minutes.
7. Select the "MATCH" button to copy the settings for Zone 2.
8. Initiate cooking by pressing the START/STOP button.
9. Flip the olives once cooked halfway through, then resume cooking.
10. Serve.

Nutrition Info:

- (Per serving) Calories 166 | Fat 3.2g |Sodium 437mg | Carbs 28.8g | Fiber 1.8g | Sugar 2.7g | Protein 5.8g

Delicious Potatoes & Carrots

Servings: 8
Cooking Time: 25 Minutes
Ingredients:
- 453g carrots, sliced
- 2 tsp smoked paprika
- 21g sugar
- 30ml olive oil
- 453g potatoes, diced
- ¼ tsp thyme
- ½ tsp dried oregano
- 1 tsp garlic powder
- Pepper
- Salt

Directions:
1. In a bowl, toss carrots and potatoes with 1 tablespoon of oil.
2. Insert a crisper plate in the Ninja Foodi air fryer baskets.
3. Add carrots and potatoes to both baskets.
4. Select zone 1 then select "air fry" mode and set the temperature to 390 degrees F for 15 minutes. Press "match" to match zone 2 settings to zone 1. Press "start/stop" to begin.
5. In a mixing bowl, add cooked potatoes, carrots, smoked paprika, sugar, oil, thyme, oregano, garlic powder, pepper, and salt and toss well.
6. Return carrot and potato mixture into the air fryer basket and cook for 10 minutes more.

Nutrition Info:
- (Per serving) Calories 101 | Fat 3.6g |Sodium 62mg | Carbs 16.6g | Fiber 3g | Sugar 5.1g | Protein 1.6g

Air Fried Okra

Servings: 2
Cooking Time: 13 Minutes.
Ingredients:
- ½ lb. okra pods sliced
- 1 teaspoon olive oil
- ¼ teaspoon salt
- ⅛ teaspoon black pepper

Directions:
1. Preheat the Ninja Foodi Dual Zone Air Fryer to 350 degrees F.
2. Toss okra with olive oil, salt, and black pepper in a bowl.
3. Spread the okra in a single layer in the two crisper plates.
4. Return the crisper plate to the Ninja Foodi Dual Zone Air Fryer.
5. Choose the Air Fry mode for Zone 1 and set the temperature to 375 degrees F and the time to 13 minutes.
6. Select the "MATCH" button to copy the settings for Zone 2.
7. Initiate cooking by pressing the START/STOP button.
8. Toss the okra once cooked halfway through, and resume cooking.
9. Serve warm.

Nutrition Info:
- (Per serving) Calories 208 | Fat 5g |Sodium 1205mg | Carbs 34.1g | Fiber 7.8g | Sugar 2.5g | Protein 5.9g

Sweet Potatoes & Brussels Sprouts

Servings: 8
Cooking Time: 35 Minutes
Ingredients:

- 340g sweet potatoes, cubed
- 30ml olive oil
- 150g onion, cut into pieces
- 352g Brussels sprouts, halved
- Pepper
- Salt
- For glaze:
- 78ml ketchup
- 115ml balsamic vinegar
- 15g mustard
- 29 ml honey

Directions:

1. In a bowl, toss Brussels sprouts, oil, onion, sweet potatoes, pepper, and salt.
2. Insert a crisper plate in the Ninja Foodi air fryer baskets.
3. Add Brussels sprouts and sweet potato mixture in both baskets.
4. Select zone 1, then select "air fry" mode and set the temperature to 390 degrees F for 25 minutes. Press "match" to match zone 2 settings to zone 1. Press "start/stop" to begin. Stir halfway through.
5. Meanwhile, add vinegar, ketchup, honey, and mustard to a saucepan and cook over medium heat for 5-10 minutes.
6. Toss cooked sweet potatoes and Brussels sprouts with sauce.

Nutrition Info:

- (Per serving) Calories 142 | Fat 4.2g | Sodium 147mg | Carbs 25.2g | Fiber 4g | Sugar 8.8g | Protein 2.9g

Fried Avocado Tacos

Servings: 4
Cooking Time: 10 Minutes
Ingredients:

- For the sauce:
- 2 cups shredded fresh kale or coleslaw mix
- ¼ cup minced fresh cilantro
- ¼ cup plain Greek yogurt
- 2 tablespoons lime juice
- 1 teaspoon honey
- ¼ teaspoon salt
- ¼ teaspoon ground chipotle pepper
- ¼ teaspoon pepper
- For the tacos:
- 1 large egg, beaten
- ¼ cup cornmeal
- ½ teaspoon salt
- ½ teaspoon garlic powder
- ½ teaspoon ground chipotle pepper
- 2 medium avocados, peeled and sliced
- Cooking spray
- 8 flour tortillas or corn tortillas (6 inches), heated up
- 1 medium tomato, chopped
- Crumbled queso fresco (optional)

Directions:

1. Combine the first 8 ingredients in a bowl. Cover and refrigerate until serving.
2. Place the egg in a shallow bowl. In another shallow bowl, mix the cornmeal, salt, garlic powder, and chipotle pepper.
3. Dip the avocado slices in the egg, then into the cornmeal mixture, gently patting to help adhere.
4. Place a crisper plate in both drawers. Put the avocado slices in the drawers in a single layer. Insert the drawers into the unit.
5. Select zone 1, then AIR FRY, then set the temperature to 360 degrees F/ 180 degrees C with a 6-minute timer. To match zone 2 settings to zone 1, choose MATCH. To begin, select START/STOP.
6. Put the avocado slices, prepared sauce, tomato, and queso fresco in the tortillas and serve.

Nutrition Info:

- (Per serving) Calories 407 | Fat 21g | Sodium 738mg | Carbs 48g | Fiber 4g | Sugar 9g | Protein 9g

Desserts Recipes

Baked Apples

Servings: 4
Cooking Time: 15 Minutes
Ingredients:
- 4 apples
- 6 teaspoons raisins
- 2 teaspoons chopped walnuts
- 2 teaspoons honey
- ½ teaspoon cinnamon

Directions:
1. Chop off the head of the apples and scoop out the flesh from the center.
2. Stuff the apples with raisins, walnuts, honey and cinnamon.
3. Place these apples in the air fryer basket 1.
4. Return the air fryer basket 1 to Zone 1 of the Ninja Foodi 2-Basket Air Fryer.
5. Choose the "Air Fry" mode for Zone 1 and set the temperature to 350 degrees F and 15 minutes of cooking time.
6. Initiate cooking by pressing the START/PAUSE BUTTON.
7. Serve.

Nutrition Info:
- (Per serving) Calories 175 | Fat 13.1g |Sodium 154mg | Carbs 14g | Fiber 0.8g | Sugar 8.9g | Protein 0.7g

Monkey Bread

Servings: 12
Cooking Time: 10 Minutes
Ingredients:
- Bread
- 12 Rhodes white dinner rolls
- ½ cup brown sugar
- 1 teaspoon cinnamon
- 4 tablespoons butter melted
- Glaze
- ½ cup powdered sugar
- 1-2 tablespoons milk
- ½ teaspoon vanilla

Directions:
1. Mix brown sugar, cinnamon and butter in a bowl.
2. Cut the dinner rolls in half and dip them in the sugar mixture.
3. Place these buns in a greased baking pan and pour the remaining butter on top.
4. Place the buns in the air fryer baskets.
5. Return the air fryer basket 1 to Zone 1, and basket 2 to Zone 2 of the Ninja Foodi 2-Basket Air Fryer.
6. Choose the "Air Fry" mode for Zone 1 at 350 degrees F and 10 minutes of cooking time.
7. Initiate cooking by pressing the START/PAUSE BUTTON.
8. Flip the rolls once cooked halfway through.
9. Meanwhile, mix milk, vanilla and sugar in a bowl.
10. Pour the glaze over the air fried rolls.
11. Serve.

Nutrition Info:
- (Per serving) Calories 192 | Fat 9.3g |Sodium 133mg | Carbs 27.1g | Fiber 1.4g | Sugar 19g | Protein 3.2g

"air-fried" Oreos Apple Fries

Servings: 4
Cooking Time: 10 Minutes

Ingredients:

- FOR THE "FRIED" OREOS
- 1 teaspoon vegetable oil
- 1 cup all-purpose flour
- 1 tablespoon granulated sugar
- 1 tablespoon baking powder
- ½ teaspoon baking soda
- ¼ teaspoon kosher salt
- 1 large egg
- ¼ cup unsweetened almond milk
- ½ teaspoon vanilla extract
- 8 Oreo cookies
- Nonstick cooking spray
- 1 tablespoon powdered sugar (optional)
- FOR THE APPLE FRIES
- 1 teaspoon vegetable oil
- 1 cup all-purpose flour
- 1 tablespoon granulated sugar
- 1 tablespoon baking powder
- ½ teaspoon baking soda
- ¼ teaspoon kosher salt
- 1 large egg
- ¼ cup unsweetened almond milk
- ½ teaspoon vanilla extract
- 2 Granny Smith apples
- 2 tablespoons cornstarch
- ½ teaspoon apple pie spice
- Nonstick cooking spray
- 1 tablespoon powdered sugar (optional)

Directions:

1. To prep the "fried" Oreos: Brush a crisper plate with the oil and install it in the Zone 1 basket.
2. In a large bowl, combine the flour, granulated sugar, baking powder, baking soda, and salt. Mix in the egg, almond milk, and vanilla to form a thick batter.
3. Using a fork or slotted spoon, dip each cookie into the batter, coating it fully. Let the excess batter drip off, then place the cookies in the prepared basket in a single layer. Spritz each with cooking spray.
4. To prep the apple fries: Brush a crisper plate with the oil and install it in the Zone 2 basket.
5. In a large bowl, combine the flour, granulated sugar, baking powder, baking soda, and salt. Mix in the egg, almond milk, and vanilla to form a thick batter.
6. Core the apples and cut them into ½-inch-thick French fry shapes. Dust lightly with the cornstarch and apple pie spice.
7. Using a fork or slotted spoon, dip each apple into the batter, coating it fully. Let the excess batter drip off, then place the apples in the prepared basket in a single layer. Spritz with cooking spray.
8. To cook the "fried" Oreos and apple fries: Insert both baskets in the unit.
9. Select Zone 1, select AIR FRY, set the temperature to 400°F, and set the timer to 8 minutes.
10. Select Zone 2, select AIR FRY, set the temperature to 400°F, and set the timer to 10 minutes. Select SMART FINISH.
11. Press START/PAUSE to begin cooking.
12. When cooking is complete, the batter will be golden brown and crisp. If desired, dust the cookies and apples with the powdered sugar before serving.

Nutrition Info:

- (Per serving) Calories: 464; Total fat: 21g; Saturated fat: 3.5g; Carbohydrates: 66g; Fiber: 2.5g; Protein: 7g; Sodium: 293mg

Walnuts Fritters

Servings: 6
Cooking Time: 15 Minutes.
Ingredients:
- 1 cup all-purpose flour
- ½ cup walnuts, chopped
- ¼ cup white sugar
- ¼ cup milk
- 1 egg
- 1 ½ teaspoons baking powder
- 1 pinch salt
- Cooking spray
- 2 tablespoons white sugar
- ½ teaspoon ground cinnamon
- Glaze:
- ½ cup confectioners' sugar
- 1 tablespoon milk
- ½ teaspoon caramel extract
- ¼ teaspoons ground cinnamon

Directions:
1. Layer both crisper plate with parchment paper.
2. Grease the parchment paper with cooking spray.
3. Whisk flour with milk, ¼ cup of sugar, egg, baking powder, and salt in a small bowl.
4. Separately mix 2 tablespoons of sugar with cinnamon in another bowl, toss in walnuts and mix well to coat.
5. Stir in flour mixture and mix until combined.
6. Drop the fritters mixture using a cookie scoop into the two crisper plate.
7. Return the crisper plate to the Ninja Foodi Dual Zone Air Fryer.
8. Choose the Air Fry mode for Zone 1 and set the temperature to 375 degrees F and the time to 15 minutes.
9. Select the "MATCH" button to copy the settings for Zone 2.
10. Initiate cooking by pressing the START/STOP button.
11. Flip the fritters once cooked halfway through, then resume cooking.
12. Meanwhile, whisk milk, caramel extract, confectioners' sugar, and cinnamon in a bowl.
13. Transfer fritters to a wire rack and allow them to cool.
14. Drizzle with a glaze over the fritters.

Nutrition Info:
- (Per serving) Calories 391 | Fat 24g |Sodium 142mg | Carbs 38.5g | Fiber 3.5g | Sugar 21g | Protein 6.6g

Oreo Rolls

Servings: 9
Cooking Time: 8 Minutes.
Ingredients:
- 1 crescent sheet roll
- 9 Oreo cookies
- Cinnamon powder, to serve
- Powdered sugar, to serve

Directions:
1. Spread the crescent sheet roll and cut it into 9 equal squares.
2. Place one cookie at the center of each square.
3. Wrap each square around the cookies and press the ends to seal.
4. Place half of the wrapped cookies in each crisper plate.
5. Return the crisper plates to the Ninja Foodi Dual Zone Air Fryer.
6. Select the Bake mode for Zone 1 and set the temperature to 360 degrees F and the time to 4-6 minutes.
7. Select the "MATCH" button to copy the settings for Zone 2.
8. Initiate cooking by pressing the START/STOP button.
9. Check for the doneness of the cookie rolls if they are golden brown, else cook 1-2 minutes more.
10. Garnish the rolls with sugar and cinnamon.
11. Serve.

Nutrition Info:
- (Per serving) Calories 175 | Fat 13.1g |Sodium 154mg | Carbs 14g | Fiber 0.8g | Sugar 8.9g | Protein 0.7g

Grilled Peaches

Servings: 2
Cooking Time: 5 Minutes
Ingredients:
- 2 yellow peaches, peeled and cut into wedges
- ¼ cup graham cracker crumbs
- ¼ cup brown sugar
- ¼ cup butter diced into tiny cubes
- Whipped cream or ice cream

Directions:
1. Toss peaches with crumbs, brown sugar, and butter in a bowl.
2. Spread the peaches in one air fryer basket.
3. Return the air fryer basket to the Ninja Foodi 2 Baskets Air Fryer.
4. Choose the "Air Fry" mode for Zone 1 and set the temperature to 350 degrees F and 5 minutes of cooking time.
5. Initiate cooking by pressing the START/PAUSE BUTTON.
6. Serve the peaches with a scoop of ice cream.

Nutrition Info:
- (Per serving) Calories 327 | Fat 14.2g |Sodium 672mg | Carbs 47.2g | Fiber 1.7g | Sugar 24.8g | Protein 4.4g

Walnut Baklava Bites Pistachio Baklava Bites

Servings:12
Cooking Time: 10 Minutes
Ingredients:
- FOR THE WALNUT BAKLAVA BITES
- ¼ cup finely chopped walnuts
- 2 teaspoons cold unsalted butter, grated
- 2 teaspoons granulated sugar
- ½ teaspoon ground cinnamon
- 6 frozen phyllo shells (from a 1.9-ounce package), thawed
- FOR THE PISTACHIO BAKLAVA BITES
- ¼ cup finely chopped pistachios
- 2 teaspoons very cold unsalted butter, grated
- 2 teaspoons granulated sugar
- ¼ teaspoon ground cardamom (optional)
- 6 frozen phyllo shells (from a 1.9-ounce package), thawed
- FOR THE HONEY SYRUP
- ¼ cup hot water
- ¼ cup honey
- 2 teaspoons fresh lemon juice

Directions:
1. To prep the walnut baklava bites: In a small bowl, combine the walnuts, butter, sugar, and cinnamon. Spoon the filling into the phyllo shells.
2. To prep the pistachio baklava bites: In a small bowl, combine the pistachios, butter, sugar, and cardamom (if using). Spoon the filling into the phyllo shells.
3. To cook the baklava bites: Install a crisper plate in each of the two baskets. Place the walnut baklava bites in the Zone 1 basket and insert the basket in the unit. Place the pistachio baklava bites in the Zone 2 basket and insert the basket in the unit.
4. Select Zone 1, select BAKE, set the temperature to 330°F, and set the timer to 10 minutes. Press MATCH COOK to match Zone 2 settings to Zone 1.
5. Press START/PAUSE to begin cooking.
6. When cooking is complete, the shells will be golden brown and crisp.
7. To make the honey syrup: In a small bowl, whisk together the hot water, honey, and lemon juice. Dividing evenly, pour the syrup over the baklava bites (you may hear a crackling sound).
8. Let cool completely before serving, about 1 hour.

Nutrition Info:
- (Per serving) Calories: 262; Total fat: 16g; Saturated fat: 3g; Carbohydrates: 29g; Fiber: 1g; Protein: 2g; Sodium: 39mg

Fudge Brownies

Servings: 4
Cooking Time: 16
Ingredients:
- 1/2 cup all-purpose flour
- 1/4 cup unsweetened cocoa powder
- 3/4 teaspoon kosher salt
- 2 large eggs, whisked
- 1 tablespoon almond milk
- 1/2 cup brown sugar
- 1/2 cup packed white sugar
- 1/2 tablespoon vanilla extract
- 8 ounces of semisweet chocolate chips, melted
- 2/4 cup unsalted butter, melted

Directions:
1. Take a medium bowl, and use a hand beater to whisk together eggs, milk, both the sugars and vanilla.
2. In a separate microwave-safe bowl, mix melted butter and chocolate and microwave it for 30 seconds to melt the chocolate.
3. Add all the listed dry ingredients to the chocolate mixture.
4. Now incorporate the egg bowl ingredient into the batter.
5. Spray a reasonable size round baking pan that fits in baskets of air fryer
6. Grease the pan with cooking spray.
7. Now pour the batter into the pan, put the crisper plate in baskets.
8. Add the pans and insert the basket into the unit.
9. Select the AIR FRY mode and adjust the setting the temperature to 300 degrees F, for 30 minutes.
10. Check it after 35 minutes and if not done, cook for 10 more minutes
11. Once it's done, take it out and let it get cool before serving.
12. Enjoy.

Nutrition Info:
- (Per serving) Calories 760| Fat43.3 g| Sodium644 mg | Carbs 93.2g | Fiber5.3 g | Sugar 70.2g | Protein 6.2g

Chocolate Cookies

Servings: 18
Cooking Time: 7 Minutes
Ingredients:
- 96g flour
- 57g butter, softened
- 15ml milk
- 7.5g cocoa powder
- 80g chocolate chips
- ½ tsp vanilla
- 35g sugar
- ¼ tsp baking soda
- Pinch of salt

Directions:
1. In a bowl, mix flour, cocoa powder, sugar, baking soda, vanilla, butter, milk, and salt until well combined.
2. Add chocolate chips and mix well.
3. Insert a crisper plate in Ninja Foodi air fryer baskets.
4. Make cookies from the mixture and place in both baskets.
5. Select zone 1 then select "air fry" mode and set the temperature to 360 degrees F for 7 minutes. Press "match" to match zone 2 settings to zone 1. Press "start/stop" to begin.

Nutrition Info:
- (Per serving) Calories 82 | Fat 4.1g |Sodium 47mg | Carbs 10.7g | Fiber 0.4g | Sugar 6.2g | Protein 1g

Jelly Donuts

Servings: 4
Cooking Time: 5 Minutes
Ingredients:
- 1 package Pillsbury Grands (Homestyle)
- ½ cup seedless raspberry jelly
- 1 tablespoon butter, melted
- ½ cup sugar

Directions:
1. Install a crisper plate in both drawers. Place half of the biscuits in the zone 1 drawer and half in zone 2's, then insert the drawers into the unit. You may need to cook in batches.
2. Select zone 1, select AIR FRY, set temperature to 390 degrees F/ 200 degrees C, and set time to 22 minutes. Select MATCH to match zone 2 settings to zone 1. Press the START/STOP button to begin cooking.
3. Place the sugar into a wide bowl with a flat bottom.
4. Baste all sides of the cooked biscuits with the melted butter and roll in the sugar to cover completely.
5. Using a long cake tip, pipe 1–2 tablespoons of raspberry jelly into each biscuit. You've now got raspberry-filled donuts!

Nutrition Info:
- (Per serving) Calories 252 | Fat 7g | Sodium 503mg | Carbs 45g | Fiber 0g | Sugar 23g | Protein 3g

Churros

Servings: 8
Cooking Time: 10 Minutes
Ingredients:
- 1 cup water
- 1/3 cup unsalted butter, cut into cubes
- 2 tablespoons granulated sugar
- ¼ teaspoon salt
- 1 cup all-purpose flour
- 2 large eggs
- 1 teaspoon vanilla extract
- Cooking oil spray
- For the cinnamon-sugar coating:
- ½ cup granulated sugar
- ¾ teaspoon ground cinnamon

Directions:
1. Add the water, butter, sugar, and salt to a medium pot. Bring to a boil over medium-high heat.
2. Reduce the heat to medium-low and stir in the flour. Cook, stirring constantly with a rubber spatula until the dough is smooth and comes together.
3. Remove the dough from the heat and place it in a mixing bowl. Allow 4 minutes for cooling.
4. In a mixing bowl, beat the eggs and vanilla extract with an electric hand mixer or stand mixer until the dough comes together. The finished product will resemble gluey mashed potatoes. Press the lumps together into a ball with your hands, then transfer to a large piping bag with a large star-shaped tip. Pipe out the churros.
5. Install a crisper plate in both drawers. Place half the churros in the zone 1 drawer and half in zone 2's, then insert the drawers into the unit.
6. Select zone 1, select AIR FRY, set temperature to 390 degrees F/ 200 degrees C, and set time to 12 minutes. Select MATCH to match zone 2 settings to zone 1. Press the START/STOP button to begin cooking.
7. In a shallow bowl, combine the granulated sugar and cinnamon.
8. Immediately transfer the baked churros to the bowl with the sugar mixture and toss to coat.

Nutrition Info:
- (Per serving) Calories 204 | Fat 9g | Sodium 91mg | Carbs 27g | Fiber 0.3g | Sugar 15g | Protein 3g

Strawberry Nutella Hand Pies

Servings: 8
Cooking Time: 10 Minutes
Ingredients:
- 1 tube pie crust dough
- 3–4 strawberries, finely chopped
- Nutella
- Sugar
- Coconut oil cooking spray

Directions:
1. Roll out the pie dough and place it on a baking sheet. Cut out hearts using a 3-inch heart-shaped cookie cutter as precisely as possible.
2. Gather the leftover dough into a ball and roll it out thinly to make a few more heart shapes. For 8 hand pies, I was able to get 16 hearts from one tube of pie crust.
3. Set aside a baking tray lined with parchment paper.
4. Spread a dollop of Nutella (approximately 1 teaspoon) on one of the hearts. Add a few strawberry pieces to the mix. Add a pinch of sugar to the top.
5. Place another heart on top and use a fork to tightly crimp the edges. Gently poke holes in the top of the pie with a fork. Place on a baking sheet. Repeat for all the pies.
6. All of the pies on the tray should be sprayed with coconut oil.
7. Install a crisper plate in both drawers. Place half the pies in the zone 1 drawer and half in zone 2's, then insert the drawers into the unit.
8. Select zone 1, select BAKE, set temperature to 390 degrees F/ 200 degrees C, and set time to 10 minutes. Select MATCH to match zone 2 settings to zone 1. Press the START/STOP button to begin cooking.

Nutrition Info:
- (Per serving) Calories 41 | Fat 2.1g | Sodium 18mg | Carbs 5.5g | Fiber 0.4g | Sugar 4.1g | Protein 0.4g

Apple Nutmeg Flautas

Servings: 8
Cooking Time: 8 Minutes.
Ingredients:
- ¼ cup light brown sugar
- ⅛ cup all-purpose flour
- ¼ teaspoon ground cinnamon
- Nutmeg, to taste
- 4 apples, peeled, cored & sliced
- ½ lemon, juice, and zest
- 6 (10-inch) flour tortillas
- Vegetable oil
- Caramel sauce
- Cinnamon sugar

Directions:
1. Mix brown sugar with cinnamon, nutmeg, and flour in a large bowl.
2. Toss in apples in lemon juice. Mix well.
3. Place a tortilla at a time on a flat surface and add ½ cup of the apple mixture to the tortilla.
4. Roll the tortilla into a burrito and seal it tightly and hold it in place with a toothpick.
5. Repeat the same steps with the remaining tortillas and apple mixture.
6. Place two apple burritos in each of the crisper plate and spray them with cooking oil.
7. Return the crisper plates to the Ninja Foodi Dual Zone Air Fryer.
8. Choose the Air Fry mode for Zone 1 and set the temperature to 400 degrees F and the time to 8 minutes.
9. Select the "MATCH" button to copy the settings for Zone 2.
10. Initiate cooking by pressing the START/STOP button.
11. Flip the burritos once cooked halfway through, then resume cooking.
12. Garnish with caramel sauce and cinnamon sugar.
13. Enjoy!

Nutrition Info:
- (Per serving) Calories 157 | Fat 1.3g | Sodium 27mg | Carbs 1.3g | Fiber 1g | Sugar 2.2g | Protein 8.2g

Dehydrated Peaches

Servings: 4
Cooking Time: 8 Hours
Ingredients:
- 300g canned peaches

Directions:
1. Insert a crisper plate in the Ninja Foodi air fryer baskets.
2. Place peaches in both baskets.
3. Select zone 1, then select "dehydrate" mode and set the temperature to 135 degrees F for 8 hours. Press "start/stop" to begin.

Nutrition Info:
- (Per serving) Calories 30 | Fat 0.2g |Sodium 0mg | Carbs 7g | Fiber 1.2g | Sugar 7g | Protein 0.7g

Air Fryer Sweet Twists

Servings: 2
Cooking Time: 9
Ingredients:
- 1 box store-bought puff pastry
- ½ teaspoon cinnamon
- ½ teaspoon sugar
- ½ teaspoon black sesame seeds
- Salt, pinch
- 2 tablespoons Parmesan cheese, freshly grated

Directions:
1. Place the dough on a work surface.
2. Take a small bowl and mix cheese, sugar, salt, sesame seeds, and cinnamon.
3. Press this mixture on both sides of the dough.
4. Now, cut the pastry into 1" x 3" strips.
5. Twist each of the strips 2 times and then lay it onto the flat.
6. Transfer to both the air fryer baskets.
7. Select zone 1 to air fry mode at 400 degrees F for 9-10 minutes.
8. Select the MATCH button for the zone 2 basket.
9. Once cooked, serve.

Nutrition Info:
- (Per serving) Calories 140| Fat9.4g| Sodium 142mg | Carbs 12.3g | Fiber0.8 g | Sugar 1.2g | Protein 2g

Brownie Muffins

Servings: 10
Cooking Time: 15 Minutes
Ingredients:
- 2 eggs
- 96g all-purpose flour
- 1 tsp vanilla
- 130g powdered sugar
- 25g cocoa powder
- 37g pecans, chopped
- 1 tsp cinnamon
- 113g butter, melted

Directions:
1. In a bowl, whisk eggs, vanilla, butter, sugar, and cinnamon until well mixed.
2. Add cocoa powder and flour and stir until well combined.
3. Add pecans and fold well.
4. Pour batter into the silicone muffin moulds.
5. Insert a crisper plate in Ninja Foodi air fryer baskets.
6. Place muffin moulds in both baskets.
7. Select zone 1, then select "bake" mode and set the temperature to 360 degrees F for 15 minutes. Press "match" and then"start/stop" to begin.

Nutrition Info:
- (Per serving) Calories 210 | Fat 10.5g |Sodium 78mg | Carbs 28.7g | Fiber 1g | Sugar 20.2g | Protein 2.6g

Dessert Empanadas

Servings: 12
Cooking Time: 10 Minutes
Ingredients:
- 12 empanada wrappers thawed
- 2 apples, chopped
- 2 tablespoons raw honey
- 1 teaspoon vanilla extract
- 1 teaspoon cinnamon
- ⅛ teaspoon nutmeg
- 2 teaspoons cornstarch
- 1 teaspoon water
- 1 egg beaten

Directions:
1. Mix apples with vanilla, honey, nutmeg, and cinnamon in a saucepan.
2. Cook for 3 minutes then mix cornstarch with water and pour into the pan.
3. Cook for 30 seconds.
4. Allow this filling to cool and keep it aside.
5. Spread the wrappers on the working surface.
6. Divide the apple filling on top of the wrappers.
7. Fold the wrappers in half and seal the edges by pressing them.
8. Brush the empanadas with the beaten egg and place them in the air fryer basket 1.
9. Return the air fryer basket 1 to Zone 1 of the Ninja Foodi 2-Basket Air Fryer.
10. Choose the "Air Fry" mode for Zone 1 at 400 degrees F and 10 minutes of cooking time.
11. Initiate cooking by pressing the START/PAUSE BUTTON.
12. Flip the empanadas once cooked halfway through.
13. Serve.

Nutrition Info:
- (Per serving) Calories 204 | Fat 9g |Sodium 91mg | Carbs 27g | Fiber 2.4g | Sugar 15g | Protein 1.3g

Cake In The Air Fryer

Servings:2
Cooking Time:30
Ingredients:
- 90 grams all-purpose flour
- Pinch of salt
- 1/2 teaspoon of baking powder
- ½ cup of tutti fruitti mix
- 2 eggs
- 1 teaspoon of vanilla extract
- 10 tablespoons of white sugar

Directions:
1. Take a bowl and add all-purpose flour, salt, and baking powder.
2. Stir it in a large bowl.
3. Whisk two eggs in a separate bowl and add vanilla extract, sugar and blend it with a hand beater.
4. Now combine wet ingredients with the dry ones.
5. Mix it well and pour it between two round pan that fits inside baskets.
6. Place the pans in both the baskets.
7. Now set the zone 1 basket to BAKE function at 310 for 30 minutes.
8. Select MATCH for zone two baskets.
9. Once it's done, serve and enjoy.

Nutrition Info:
- (Per serving) Calories 711| Fat4.8g| Sodium 143mg | Carbs 161g | Fiber 1.3g | Sugar 105g | Protein 10.2g

Lemon Sugar Cookie Bars Monster Sugar Cookie Bars

Servings: 12
Cooking Time: 18 Minutes
Ingredients:
- FOR THE LEMON COOKIE BARS
- Grated zest and juice of 1 lemon
- ½ cup granulated sugar
- 4 tablespoons (½ stick) unsalted butter, at room temperature
- 1 large egg yolk
- 1 teaspoon vanilla extract
- ⅛ teaspoon baking powder
- ½ cup plus 2 tablespoons all-purpose flour
- FOR THE MONSTER COOKIE BARS
- ½ cup granulated sugar
- 4 tablespoons (½ stick) unsalted butter, at room temperature
- 1 large egg yolk
- 1 teaspoon vanilla extract
- ⅛ teaspoon baking powder
- ½ cup plus 2 tablespoons all-purpose flour
- ¼ cup rolled oats
- ¼ cup M&M's
- ¼ cup peanut butter chips

Directions:
1. To prep the lemon cookie bars: In a large bowl, rub together the lemon zest and sugar. Add the butter and use a hand mixer to beat until light and fluffy.
2. Beat in the egg yolk, vanilla, and lemon juice. Mix in the baking powder and flour.
3. To prep the monster cookie bars: In a large bowl, with a hand mixer, beat the sugar and butter until light and fluffy.
4. Beat in the egg yolk and vanilla. Mix in the baking powder and flour. Stir in the oats, M&M's, and peanut butter chips.
5. To cook the cookie bars: Line both baskets with aluminum foil. Press the lemon cookie dough into the Zone 1 basket and insert the basket in the unit. Press the monster cookie dough into the Zone 2 basket and insert the basket in the unit.
6. Select Zone 1, select BAKE, set the temperature to 330°F, and set the timer to 18 minutes. Press MATCH COOK to match Zone 2 settings to Zone 1.
7. Press START/PAUSE to begin cooking.
8. When cooking is complete, the cookies should be set in the middle and have begun to pull away from the sides of the basket.
9. Let the cookies cool completely, about 1 hour. Cut each basket into 6 bars for a total of 12 bars.

Nutrition Info:
- (Per serving) Calories: 191; Total fat: 8.5g; Saturated fat: 5g; Carbohydrates: 27g; Fiber: 0.5g; Protein: 2g; Sodium: 3mg

Cinnamon Bread Twists

Servings: 4
Cooking Time: 15 Minutes
Ingredients:
- Bread Twists Dough
- 120g all-purpose flour
- 1 teaspoon baking powder
- ¼ teaspoon salt
- 150g fat free Greek yogurt
- Brushing
- 2 tablespoons light butter
- 2 tablespoons granulated sugar
- 1-2 teaspoons ground cinnamon, to taste

Directions:
1. Mix flour, salt and baking powder in a bowl.
2. Stir in yogurt and the rest of the dough ingredients in a bowl.
3. Mix well and make 8 inches long strips out of this dough.
4. Twist the strips and place them in the air fryer baskets.
5. Return the air fryer basket 1 to Zone 1, and basket 2 to Zone 2 of the Ninja Foodi 2-Basket Air Fryer.
6. Choose the "Air Fry" mode for Zone 1 at 375 degrees F and 15 minutes of cooking time.
7. Select the "MATCH COOK" option to copy the settings for Zone 2.
8. Initiate cooking by pressing the START/PAUSE BUTTON.
9. Flip the twists once cooked halfway through.
10. Mix butter with cinnamon and sugar in a bowl.
11. Brush this mixture over the twists.
12. Serve.

Nutrition Info:
- (Per serving) Calories 391 | Fat 24g | Sodium 142mg | Carbs 38.5g | Fiber 3.5g | Sugar 21g | Protein 6.6g

Lava Cake

Servings: 4
Cooking Time: 10 Minutes

Ingredients:

- 1 cup semi-sweet chocolate chips
- 8 tablespoons butter
- 4 eggs
- 2 teaspoons vanilla extract
- ½ teaspoon salt
- 6 tablespoons all-purpose flour
- 1 cup powdered sugar
- For the chocolate filling:
- 2 tablespoons Nutella
- 1 tablespoon butter, softened
- 1 tablespoon powdered sugar

Directions:

1. Heat the chocolate chips and butter in a medium-sized microwave-safe bowl in 30-second intervals until thoroughly melted and smooth, stirring after each interval.
2. Whisk together the eggs, vanilla, salt, flour, and powdered sugar in a mixing bowl.
3. Combine the Nutella, softened butter, and powdered sugar in a separate bowl.
4. Spray 4 ramekins with oil and fill them halfway with the chocolate chip mixture. Fill each ramekin halfway with Nutella, then top with the remaining chocolate chip mixture, making sure the Nutella is well covered.
5. Install a crisper plate in both drawers. Place 2 ramekins in each drawer and insert the drawers into the unit.
6. Select zone 1, select AIR FRY, set temperature to 390 degrees F/ 200 degrees C, and set time to 22 minutes. Select MATCH to match zone 2 settings to zone 1. Press the START/STOP button to begin cooking.
7. Serve hot.

Nutrition Info:

- (Per serving) Calories 338 | Fat 21.2g | Sodium 1503mg | Carbs 5.1g | Fiber 0.3g | Sugar 4.6g | Protein 29.3g

Cinnamon-sugar "churros" With Caramel Sauce

Servings:4
Cooking Time: 10 Minutes

Ingredients:

- FOR THE "CHURROS"
- 1 sheet frozen puff pastry, thawed
- Butter-flavored cooking spray
- 1 tablespoon granulated sugar
- 1 teaspoon ground cinnamon
- FOR THE CARAMEL SAUCE
- ½ cup packed light brown sugar
- 2 tablespoons unsalted butter, cut into small pieces
- ¼ cup heavy (whipping) cream
- 2 teaspoons vanilla extract
- ⅛ teaspoon kosher salt

Directions:

1. To prep the "churros": Cut the puff pastry crosswise into 4 rectangles. Fold each piece in half lengthwise to make a long thin "churro."
2. To prep the caramel sauce: Measure the brown sugar, butter, cream, and vanilla into an ovenproof ramekin or bowl (no need to stir).
3. To cook the "churros" and caramel sauce: Install a crisper plate in the Zone 1 basket. Place the "churros" in the basket and insert the basket in the unit. Place the ramekin in the Zone 2 basket and insert the basket in the unit.
4. Select Zone 1, select AIR FRY, set the temperature to 330°F, and set the timer to 10 minutes.
5. Select Zone 2, select BAKE, set the temperature to 350°F, and set the timer to 10 minutes. Select SMART FINISH.
6. Press START/PAUSE to begin cooking.
7. When the Zone 2 timer reads 5 minutes, press START/PAUSE. Remove the basket and stir the caramel. Reinsert the basket and press START/PAUSE to resume cooking.
8. When cooking is complete, the "churros" will be golden brown and cooked through and the caramel sauce smooth.
9. Spritz each "churro" with cooking spray and sprinkle generously with the granulated sugar and cinnamon.
10. Stir the salt into the caramel sauce. Let cool for 5 to 10 minutes before serving. Note that the caramel will thicken as it cools.

Nutrition Info:

- (Per serving) Calories: 460; Total fat: 26g; Saturated fat: 14g; Carbohydrates: 60g; Fiber: 1.5g; Protein: 5g; Sodium: 254mg

Apple Fritters

Servings: 14
Cooking Time: 10 Minutes
Ingredients:

- 2 large apples
- 2 cups all-purpose flour
- ½ cup granulated sugar
- 1 tablespoon baking powder
- 1 teaspoon salt
- 1 teaspoon ground cinnamon
- ½ teaspoon ground nutmeg
- ¼ teaspoon ground cloves
- ¾ cup apple cider or apple juice
- 2 eggs
- 3 tablespoons butter, melted
- 1 teaspoon vanilla extract
- For the apple cider glaze:
- 2 cups powdered sugar
- ¼ cup apple cider or apple juice
- ½ teaspoon ground cinnamon
- ¼ teaspoon ground nutmeg

Directions:
1. Peel and core the apples, then cut them into ¼-inch cubes. Spread the apple chunks out on a kitchen towel to absorb any excess moisture.
2. In a mixing bowl, combine the flour, sugar, baking powder, salt, and spices.
3. Add the apple chunks and combine well.
4. Whisk together the apple cider, eggs, melted butter, and vanilla in a small bowl.
5. Combine the wet and dry ingredients in a large mixing bowl.
6. Install a crisper plate in both drawers. Use an ice cream scoop to scoop 3 to 4 dollops of fritter dough into the zone 1 drawer and 3 to 4 dollops into the zone 2 drawer. Insert the drawers into the unit. You may need to cook in batches.
7. Select zone 1, select BAKE, set temperature to 390 degrees F/ 200 degrees C, and set time to 10 minutes. Select MATCH to match zone 2 settings to zone 1. Press the START/STOP button to begin cooking.
8. Meanwhile, make the glaze: Whisk the powdered sugar, apple cider, and spices together until smooth.
9. When the fritters are cooked, drizzle the glaze over them. Let sit for 10 minutes until the glaze sets.

Nutrition Info:
- (Per serving) Calories 221 | Fat 3g | Sodium 288mg | Carbs 46g | Fiber 2g | Sugar 29g | Protein 3g

Blueberry Pie Egg Rolls

Servings: 12
Cooking Time: 5 Minutes
Ingredients:

- 12 egg roll wrappers
- 2 cups of blueberries
- 1 tablespoon of cornstarch
- ½ cup of agave nectar
- 1 teaspoon of lemon zest
- 2 tablespoons of water
- 1 tablespoon of lemon juice
- Olive oil or butter flavored cooking spray
- Confectioner's sugar for dusting

Directions:
1. Mix blueberries with cornstarch, lemon zest, agave and water in a saucepan.
2. Cook this mixture for 5 minutes on a simmer.
3. Allow the mixture to cool.
4. Spread the roll wrappers and divide the filling at the center of the wrappers.
5. Fold the two edges and roll each wrapper.
6. Wet and seal the wrappers then place them in the air fryer basket 1.
7. Spray these rolls with cooking spray.
8. Return the air fryer basket 1 to Zone 1 of the Ninja Foodi 2-Basket Air Fryer.
9. Choose the "Air Fry" mode for Zone 1 at 350 degrees F and 5 minutes of cooking time.
10. Initiate cooking by pressing the START/PAUSE BUTTON.
11. Dust the rolls with confectioner' sugar.
12. Serve.

Nutrition Info:
- (Per serving) Calories 258 | Fat 12.4g | Sodium 79mg | Carbs 34.3g | Fiber 1g | Sugar 17g | Protein 3.2g

Appendix : Recipes Index

"air-fried" Oreos Apple Fries 81
"fried" Fish With Seasoned Potato Wedges 61

A

Acorn Squash Slices 71
Air Fried Okra 78
Air Fryer Sausage Patties 9
Air Fryer Sweet Twists 87
Air-fried Radishes 75
Apple Fritters 91
Apple Nutmeg Flautas 86
Avocado Fries With Sriracha Dip 28

B

Bacon And Egg Omelet 14
Bacon And Eggs For Breakfast 8
Bacon Wrapped Corn Cob 75
Bacon Wrapped Tater Tots 22
Bagels 13
Baked Apples 80
Baked Mushroom And Mozzarella Frittata With Breakfast Potatoes 7
Balsamic Duck Breast 47
Balsamic Steak Tips With Roasted Asparagus And Mushroom Medley 36
Banana And Raisins Muffins 6
Bang-bang Chicken 53
Bbq Cheddar-stuffed Chicken Breasts 45
Bbq Pork Chops 40
Beef Ribs I 33
Beef Ribs Ii 38
Blackened Mahimahi With Honey-roasted Carrots 57
Blueberry Coffee Cake And Maple Sausage Patties 15
Blueberry Pie Egg Rolls 91
Breakfast Bacon 12
Breakfast Casserole 14
Breakfast Potatoes 7
Breakfast Sausage Omelet 11
Broccoli, Squash, & Pepper 76
Broiled Teriyaki Salmon With Eggplant In Stir-fry Sauce 59
Brownie Muffins 87
Buffalo Seitan With Crispy Zucchini Noodles 71

Buttered Mahi-mahi 55

C

Cake In The Air Fryer 88
Cauliflower Cheese Patties 18
Cheesy Potatoes With Asparagus 72
Chicken & Veggies 51
Chicken And Potatoes 45
Chicken Leg Piece 50
Chicken Parmesan 47
Chicken Tenders 18
Chickpea Fritters 74
Chili-lime Crispy Chickpeas Pizza-seasoned Crispy Chickpeas 24
Chocolate Cookies 84
Churros 85
Cilantro Lime Steak 32
Cinnamon Bread Twists 89
Cinnamon Sugar Chickpeas 22
Cinnamon Toasts 13
Cinnamon-raisin Bagels Everything Bagels 5
Cinnamon-sugar "churros" With Caramel Sauce 90
Cornish Hen 46
Crab Cake Poppers 28
Crab Cakes 25
Crab Rangoon Dip With Crispy Wonton Strips 27
Crispy Chickpeas 23
Crispy Fish Nuggets 59
Crispy Parmesan Cod 60
Crispy Plantain Chips 20
Curry-crusted Lamb Chops With Baked Brown Sugar Acorn Squash 34

D

Dehydrated Peaches 87
Delicious Potatoes & Carrots 78
Dessert Empanadas 88
Donuts 17
Dried Apple Chips Dried Banana Chips 21

E

Egg With Baby Spinach 16

F

Falafel 73
Fish Tacos 65
Flavorful Salmon With Green Beans 58
Fried Artichoke Hearts 70
Fried Avocado Tacos 79
Fried Olives 77
Fried Tilapia 62
Frozen Breaded Fish Fillet 57
Fudge Brownies 84

G

Garlic Potato Wedges In Air Fryer 68
Garlic Shrimp With Pasta Alfredo 62
General Tso's Chicken 49
Glazed Scallops 60
Glazed Thighs With French Fries 43
Goat Cheese–stuffed Chicken Breast With Broiled Zucchini And Cherry Tomatoes 52
Green Beans With Baked Potatoes 73
Green Salad With Crispy Fried Goat Cheese And Baked Croutons 70
Green Tomato Stacks 68
Grill Cheese Sandwich 23
Grilled Peaches 83

H

Ham Burger Patties 35
Hasselback Potatoes 76
Honey-cajun Chicken Thighs 52

I

Italian Chicken & Potatoes 44

J

Jalapeño Popper Chicken 27
Jalapeño Popper Dip With Tortilla Chips 29
Jelly Donuts 85
Juicy Duck Breast 49

K

Kale And Spinach Chips 77
Kale Potato Nuggets 19
Korean Bbq Beef 34

L

Lamb Chops With Dijon Garlic 38
Lamb Shank With Mushroom Sauce 30
Lava Cake 90
Lemon Herb Cauliflower 72
Lemon Pepper Fish Fillets 63
Lemon Sugar Cookie Bars Monster Sugar Cookie Bars 89
Lime Glazed Tofu 74

M

Mac And Cheese Balls 20
Marinated Chicken Legs 43
Marinated Pork Chops 32
Mongolian Beef With Sweet Chili Brussels Sprouts 41
Monkey Bread 80
Morning Egg Rolls 9
Mozzarella Balls 29

O

Onion Rings 21
Oreo Rolls 82

P

Paprika Pork Chops 39
Parmesan Crush Chicken 25
Parmesan French Fries 19
Parmesan-crusted Fish Sticks With Baked Macaroni And Cheese 56
Perfect Cinnamon Toast 12
Pickled Chicken Fillets 54
Pork Chops And Potatoes 31
Pork Chops With Apples 31
Pork Chops With Brussels Sprouts 42
Pork Katsu With Seasoned Rice 37
Pork Tenderloin With Brown Sugar–pecan Sweet Potatoes 30
Pork With Green Beans And Potatoes 40
Potatoes & Beans 75
Pumpkin French Toast Casserole With Sweet And Spicy Twisted Bacon 11

R

Ranch Turkey Tenders With Roasted Vegetable Salad 46
Roasted Garlic Chicken Pizza With Cauliflower "wings" 53
Roasted Oranges 15

S

Salmon With Green Beans 55
Sausage & Butternut Squash 8
Sausage Meatballs 36
Savory Salmon Fillets 61
Scallops 64
Shrimp Po'boys With Sweet Potato Fries 67
Shrimp Skewers 58
Shrimp With Lemon And Pepper 56
Southwestern Fish Fillets 63
Spicy Chicken 54
Spicy Chicken Wings 51
Spicy Salmon Fillets 58
Spinach And Red Pepper Egg Cups With Coffee-glazed Canadian Bacon 17
Steak And Asparagus Bundles 39
Strawberry Baked Oats Chocolate Peanut Butter Baked Oats 10
Strawberry Nutella Hand Pies 86
Strip Steaks With Hasselback Potatoes 33
Stuffed Bell Peppers 26
Sweet Potato Hash 6
Sweet Potatoes & Brussels Sprouts 79

T

Tasty Pork Skewers 42
Tater Tots 24
Thai Chicken Meatballs 44
Tilapia With Mojo And Crispy Plantains 66
Tofu Veggie Meatballs 26
Tuna Patties 64

V

Veggie Burgers With "fried" Onion Rings 69
Veggie Stuffed Chicken Breasts 48

W

Walnut Baklava Bites Pistachio Baklava Bites 83
Walnuts Fritters 82
Wings With Corn On Cob 48

Y

Yellow Potatoes With Eggs 10
Yogurt Lamb Chops 35
Yummy Chicken Breasts 50

DRONES

Deep-Sea Drones

BY MARTHA LONDON

CONTENT CONSULTANT
MICHAEL BRAASCH, PHD, PE
THOMAS PROFESSOR OF ELECTRICAL ENGINEERING
OHIO UNIVERSITY

Kids Core
An Imprint of Abdo Publishing
abdobooks.com

abdobooks.com

Published by Abdo Publishing, a division of ABDO, PO Box 398166, Minneapolis, Minnesota 55439. Copyright © 2021 by Abdo Consulting Group, Inc. International copyrights reserved in all countries. No part of this book may be reproduced in any form without written permission from the publisher. Kids Core™ is a trademark and logo of Abdo Publishing.

Printed in the United States of America, North Mankato, Minnesota
082020
012021

THIS BOOK CONTAINS RECYCLED MATERIALS

Cover Photo: Kryvenok Anastasiia/Shutterstock Images
Interior Photos: Sofar Ocean, 4–5; Niklas Larsson/AP Images, 7; Jim Bovin/AP Images, 8; Vismar UK/Shutterstock Images, 10; Photopqr/La Provence/Maxppp/Newscom, 12–13; NOAA/OAR/OER, 15; Ross D. Franklin/AP Images, 16; Emory Kristof/National Geographic, 18–19; Zhang Xudong/Xinhua News Agency/Newscom, 21, 29 (top); Chine Nouvelle/SIPA/Newscom, 22; National Oceanography Centre/dpa/picture-alliance/Newscom, 24, 25, 29 (bottom); Robosea/Cover Images/Newscom, 26; Bettmann/Getty Images, 28

Editor: Maddie Spalding
Series Designer: Katharine Hale

Library of Congress Control Number: 2019954082

Publisher's Cataloging-in-Publication Data

Names: London, Martha, author
Title: Deep-sea drones / by Martha London
Description: Minneapolis, Minnesota : Abdo Publishing, 2021 | Series: Drones | Includes online resources and index.
Identifiers: ISBN 9781532192784 (lib. bdg.) | ISBN 9781644944387 (pbk.) | ISBN 9781098210687 (ebook)
Subjects: LCSH: Deep diving vehicles--Juvenile literature. | Deep submergence vehicles--Juvenile literature. | Remotely controlled underwater vehicles--Juvenile literature. | Ocean exploration--Juvenile literature. | Deep diving--Equipment and supplies--Juvenile literature.
Classification: DDC 623.8205--dc23

CONTENTS

CHAPTER 1
Exploring a Shipwreck 4

CHAPTER 2
Drones at Work 12

CHAPTER 3
Then and Now 18

Drone Stats 28
Glossary 30
Online Resources 31
Learn More 31
Index 32
About the Author 32

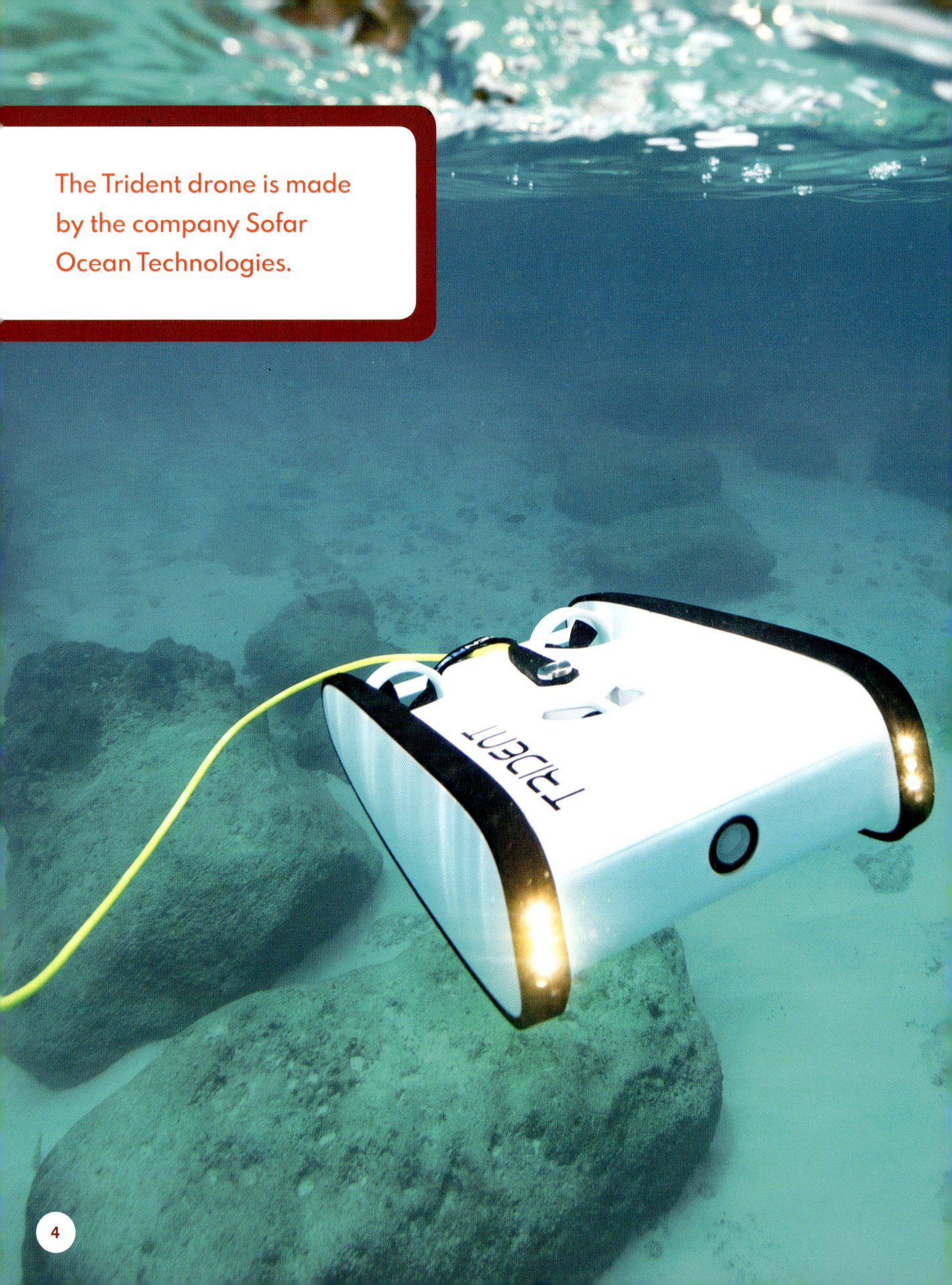

The Trident drone is made by the company Sofar Ocean Technologies.

CHAPTER 1

Exploring a Shipwreck

It is June 2016. Two people sit in a boat on Lake Tahoe in Nevada. They lower a Trident drone into the lake. The drone's mission is to explore the SS *Tahoe*. The SS *Tahoe* was a steamship. It now lies about 400 feet (120 m) below the lake's surface.

The SS *Tahoe* is 169 feet (52 m) long. It carried passengers and delivered mail in the early 1900s. It sank in 1940.

The drone dives. It has a camera that films live video. The drone's lights shine into the darkness. Rusted metal appears. The drone follows the path of a deck. Inside a doorway sits a sink once used to wash sailors' hands.

The Deep Ocean

The **pressure** at the bottom of the ocean is very high. Scientists cannot explore the bottom layers of the ocean easily. A scuba diver can reach depths of 130 feet (40 m). Most divers do not go deeper than that. It is not safe. But the pressure does not harm deep-sea drones.

Drone operators use special equipment to steer and control the drones.

Crumpled **stacks** rise from the middle of the deck. Steam from the engine once puffed up and out of the stacks.

The *Argus* drone is large. It explores shipwrecks.

Types of Drones

Drones are special machines that are often used for exploration. Deep-sea drones dive to underwater places people cannot get to. Scientists use these drones to study lakes and oceans. Drones help them learn more about underwater animals.

There are two main types of underwater drones. Some drones are controlled by people. These are called remotely operated vehicles (ROVs). **Autonomous** underwater vehicles (AUVs) dive without human control. There are benefits to each. Scientists can choose what to pick up with an ROV. But an ROV has a long cord called a tether. The tether connects the drone to a boat or ship at the surface.

Diagram of an ROV

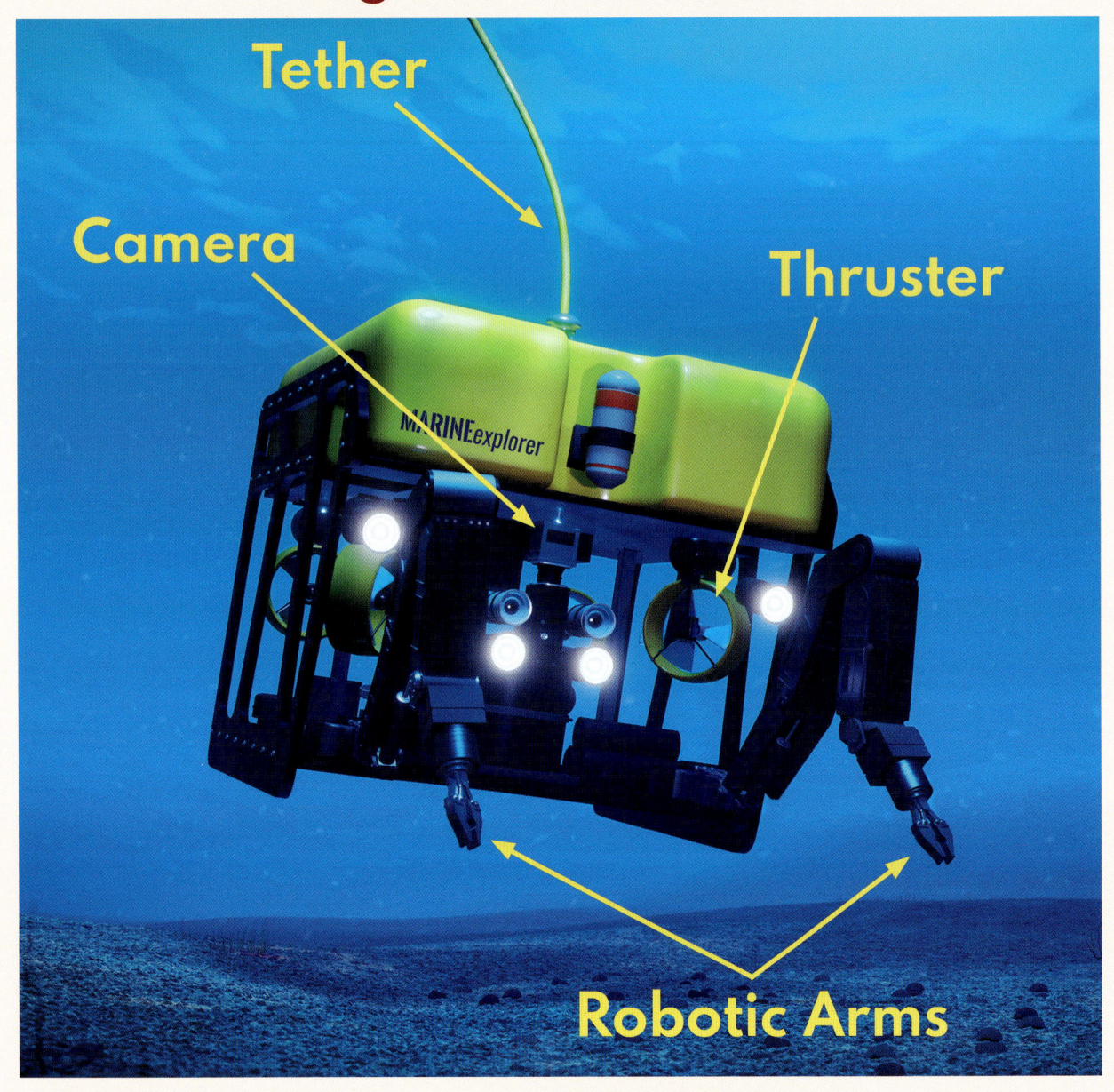

Tether

Camera

Thruster

Robotic Arms

This diagram shows the parts of an ROV. Each part has a different function. Robotic arms help the drone pick things up. Thrusters help the drone move.

Scientists use the tether to communicate with the drone. AUVs do not need tethers. They can dive and steer on their own.

Drones have many uses. They can take video and pictures. People use drones to understand the world.

Further Evidence

Look at the website below. Does it give any new evidence to support the information in Chapter One?

Listening to the Ocean

abdocorelibrary.com/deep-sea-drones

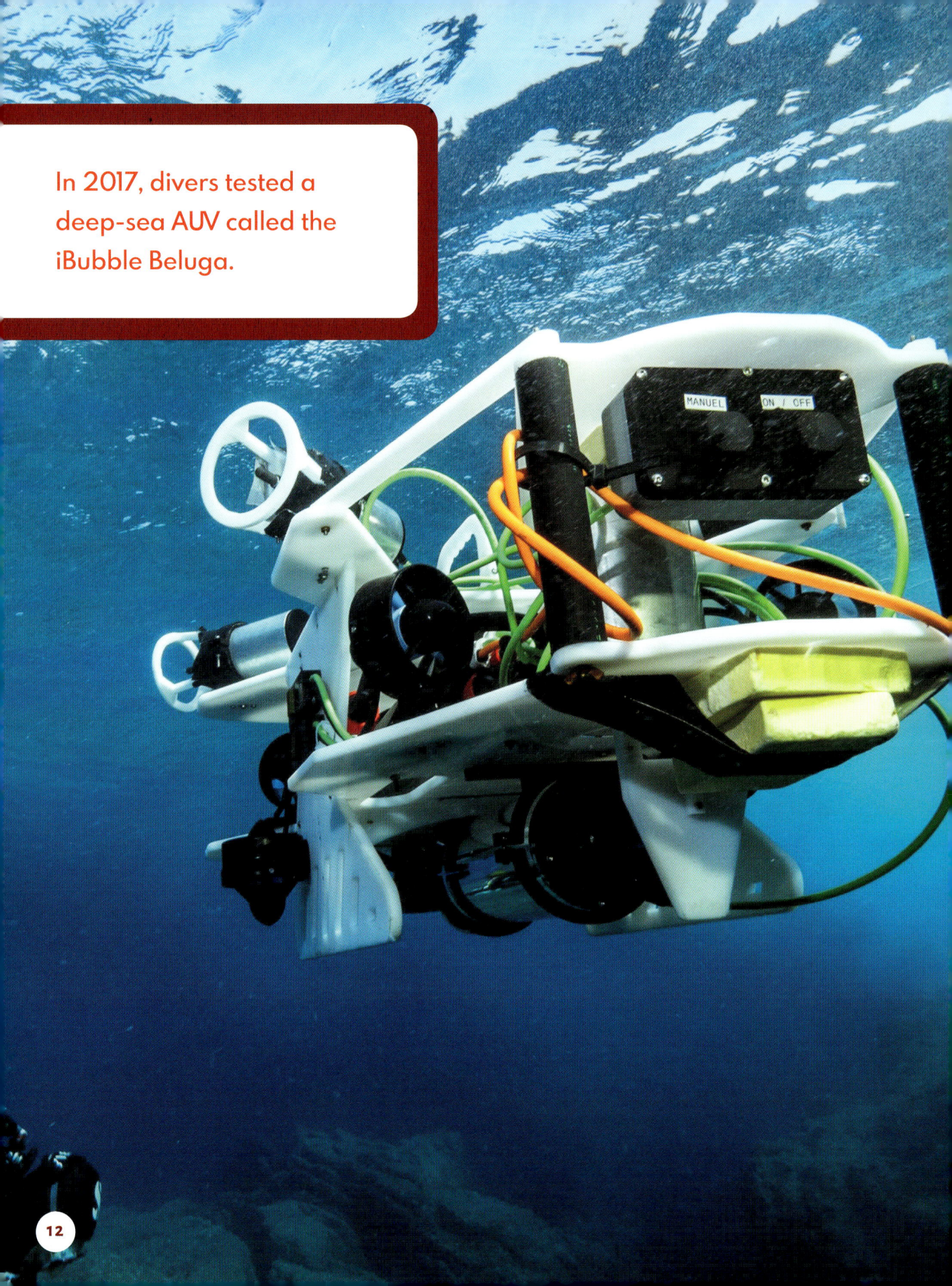

In 2017, divers tested a deep-sea AUV called the iBubble Beluga.

CHAPTER **2**

Drones at Work

Scientists do not know much about the ocean floor. Humans have only explored about 5 percent of it. Deep-sea drones are important scientific tools. They can map the seafloor. They use technology to build a picture of what the seafloor looks like.

For example, some drones use sound waves. Sound travels in waves. Drones emit a sound. They measure how long it takes the sound wave to bounce from the floor back to the machine. Scientists use these measurements to find changes in depth.

Drones also measure the water's temperature. Some parts of the ocean have **vents**. Vents are large cracks in the ocean floor. They release very hot water. Scientists want to

Mapping the Seafloor

Scientists want to build teams of drones. The drones could work together to map large sections of the ocean floor. The map would show what the ocean floor looks like. Scientists could also learn what it is made of.

Some drones take rock samples from ocean vents to learn more about deep-sea habitats.

learn how tiny **organisms** survive in the vents. Drones could help them learn more about these organisms.

Other Uses

People use drones for other jobs too. For example, ship captains sometimes use drones. Drones take photos of the bottoms of ships. They also photograph nets. Captains can look at the drone's pictures to see if repairs are needed.

Some small ROVs can be controlled by smartphones.

Even people who are not scientists use drones. People can only dive up to a certain depth. Drones can help them explore bodies of water.

Primary Source

Tim Shank studies ocean life. He explained why scientists want to explore the deepest parts of the ocean:

> *We have some [basic] questions about who lives there. . . . This is an area over half the size of Australia that we haven't explored yet.*

Source: Mark Kaufman. "NASA Dropped a Space Exploration Robot into Cape Cod's Waters to Reach the Darkest Unknowns." *Mashable*, 1 Mar. 2019, mashable.com. Accessed 27 Aug. 2019.

What's the Big Idea?

Read this quote carefully. What is its main idea? Explain how the main idea is supported by details.

In the mid-1990s, a film crew explored the wreck of the RMS *Titanic* to make the 1997 movie *Titanic*.

CHAPTER 3

Then and Now

Scientists have used drones for many years. One of the most famous examples is an ROV called *Argo*. In 1985, *Argo* discovered the lost passenger ship RMS *Titanic*. The *Titanic* sank near Newfoundland in 1912.

A tether connected *Argo* to a boat at the surface. The tether powered the drone. *Argo* had video cameras and lights. The research team used the drone to map the shipwreck. *Argo* was 15 feet (5 m) long. It weighed more than 4,000 pounds (1,800 kg).

The *Titanic* was not the only famous shipwreck that *Argo* found. In 1989, the drone found a lost World War II (1939–1945) battleship off the coast of France. By exploring shipwrecks, drones can help researchers understand the past.

The Mariana Trench

Drones are going places scientists were not sure could be explored. For example, the ROV

Chinese scientists created the *Discovery* ROV.

Discovery explored the Mariana Trench in 2019. A trench is a long and narrow hole in the seafloor. The Mariana Trench is on the floor of the western North Pacific Ocean.

The *Discovery* took pictures of colorful corals that live near the Mariana Trench.

The Mariana Trench is more than 1,580 miles (2,540 km) long. It has the deepest point on Earth. It is nearly 7 miles (11 km) below the ocean's surface.

A tether connected the *Discovery* to a ship at the ocean's surface. The drone dove deep into the Mariana Trench. It took pictures and video of organisms that lived there. It streamed the pictures and video to computers on the ship. Scientists studied the ocean life the drone found.

Personal Drones

Research drones are often large. Personal drones are usually smaller. For example, the iBubble is an AUV people can buy. It is only 19 pounds (9 kg). It uses special technology. The technology helps the drone avoid objects such as coral. iBubble can follow divers and take video.

Scientists at the National Oceanography Centre in Southampton, United Kingdom, created the *Boaty McBoatface* AUV.

Exploring Polar Oceans

Another research drone scientists have developed is the AUV *Boaty McBoatface*. *Boaty* is a submarine. Researchers use *Boaty* to study warming waters in Earth's polar oceans.

Boaty can travel hundreds of miles and cover a wide area.

Oceans are heating up due to global warming. Global warming is an increase in temperatures worldwide. It is caused by heat getting trapped in Earth's **atmosphere**.

The BIKI has a tail fin that steers the drone. This ROV can be controlled wirelessly through a phone app.

Drones of the Future

Researchers are always working to improve underwater drones. They are making drones smaller and lighter. Researchers are also creating drones that are quieter in the water. That way, animals are not afraid of the drones. They do not get scared and swim away. This allows scientists to see more marine life. These are the drones of the future.

Explore Online

Visit the website below. Did you learn any new information about deep-sea drones that wasn't in Chapter Three?

Drones in the Antarctic

abdocorelibrary.com/deep-sea-drones

Drone Stats

Argo

- ROV
- More than 4,000 pounds (1,800 kg)
- Found and explored the sunken ship the *Titanic*

Discovery

- ROV
- Explored the Mariana Trench
- Took pictures and video of animals that live in the deepest parts of the ocean

Boaty McBoatface

- AUV
- Used to study polar oceans

Glossary

atmosphere
the layer of gases that separates the surface of a planet from space

autonomous
able to operate without a person controlling it

organisms
living things

pressure
the force of weight on an object

stacks
tall columns that allow steam from an engine to escape

vents
openings where gas or liquid escapes

Online Resources

To learn more about deep-sea drones, visit our free resource websites below.

Core Library CONNECTION
FREE! COMMON CORE MULTIMEDIA RESOURCES

Visit **abdocorelibrary.com** or scan this QR code for free Common Core resources for teachers and students, including vetted activities, multimedia, and booklinks, for deeper subject comprehension.

Booklinks NONFICTION NETWORK
FREE! ONLINE NONFICTION RESOURCES

Visit **abdobooklinks.com** or scan this QR code for free additional online weblinks for further learning. These links are routinely monitored and updated to provide the most current information available.

Learn More

Abell, Tracy, and Alexis Roumanis. *Drones.* AV2 by Weigl, 2019.

Howell, Izzi. *Drones.* Franklin Watts, 2019.

Watts, Pam. *Ocean Ecosystems.* Abdo Publishing, 2016.

Index

Argo, 19–20
autonomous underwater vehicles (AUVs), 9, 11, 23, 24

Boaty McBoatface, 24

Discovery, 21, 23

iBubble, 23

Mariana Trench, 20–23

ocean vents, 14–15
organisms, 15, 23

remotely operated vehicles (ROVs), 9, 10, 19–21, 23
research drones, 19–20, 23, 24–25, 27
RMS *Titanic*, 19–20

shipwrecks, 5–7, 19–20
SS *Tahoe*, 5–7

Trident drone, 5–6

About the Author

Martha London writes books for young readers full-time. When she isn't writing, you can find her hiking in the woods.